Alexa

City of Gifts and Sorrows

To Jean

Alexandria

City of Gifts and Sorrows

FROM HELLENISTIC CIVILIZATION TO MULTIETHNIC METROPOLIS

A. J. POLYZOIDES

June 24th 2017

To Patou,

I am thrilled that you read my book, about my birthplace until I left the city and settled in England falling in love with the people, the NHS and orthopaedics. Love & admiration

John P.

sussex
ACADEMIC
PRESS

Brighton • Chicago • Toronto

Pat.
Carry on being the lovely person you are — stay healthy! x Jean

2 4 6 8 10 9 7 5 3 1

First published 2014, in Great Britain by
SUSSEX ACADEMIC PRESS
PO Box 139
Eastbourne BN24 9BP

SUSSEX ACADEMIC PRESS
Independent Publishers Group
814 N. Franklin Street, Chicago, IL 60610

and in Canada by
SUSSEX ACADEMIC PRESS (CANADA)
1108 / 115 Antibes Drive, Toronto, Ontario M2R 2Y9

British Library Cataloguing in Publication Data
A CIP catalogue record for this book is available from the British Library.

Library of Congress Cataloging-in-Publication Data
Polyzoides, Apostolos, author.
Alexandria : city of gifts and sorrows : from Hellenistic civilization to multiethnic metropolis / Apostolos Polyzoides.
pages   cm
Includes bibliographical references and index.
ISBN 978-1-84519-667-7 (pbk : alk. paper)
   1. Alexandria (Egypt)—History. I. Title.
DT154.A4P66 2014
962.1—dc23

2014017867

MIX
Paper from
responsible sources
FSC
www.fsc.org   FSC® C013056

Typeset & designed by Sussex Academic Press, Brighton & Eastbourne.
Printed TJ International, Padstow, Cornwall.

Contents

Preface

Fortunate is he who has studied history.

Euripides 480–407 BCE

Over the centuries, historians, scholars and writers have consistently neglected the history of ancient Alexandria in Egypt – the renowned city of the 3rd century BCE, birthplace of science and the modern mind – in comparison to the numerous books on pharaonic Egypt, Athens and Rome. The aim of this book is to reveal the real history of ancient and modern Alexandria, and to record its importance to western culture.

During my student days, I walked along its coastal promenade, avenues and narrow alleyways, perplexed at the absence of Greek Ptolemaic archaeological remains, whose civilisation lasted for three hundred years.

It is surreal, but also fascinating, that Alexander the Great – having conquered Asia Minor, Persia, Babylon and going as far as India – chose a desolate plot of land on the Mediterranean coast in Egypt, opposite the island of Pharos, to build his capital. Homer, in the 8th century BCE, used the word *histor* to describe a person who passed judgement on facts after an enquiry. The recording of history started in Greece, with Herodotus and Thucydides in the 5th century BCE. Ancient and modern historians presented past events either as a pure narrative or as a timeless analysis of events. A different approach is used in this book, by presenting the relevant historical events from the rise to the fall of a city, the achievements during its apogee, and the reasons for its decline and collapse. Alexandrian history was shaped by the Ptolemies in the 3rd century BCE – there was no city in the world that could claim to have been built, in less than half a century, with a lighthouse, Grand Library and Museum (which functioned as a university), the Serapeion temple, one deity for both Greeks and Egyptians, and a trading centre: the Emporium.

In 30 BCE, Octavian invaded Alexandria and ruled Egypt and the East. When the power of the Roman army was declining, the Arabs were expanding, and they occupied Alexandria without any resistance in 645 CE. Under the Arabs, Alexandria continued to be a trading centre with other western countries in North Africa. In 1517 CE, the Turks occupied Egypt but neglected Alexandria, and it was under their rule that the great ancient city was reduced to a small fishing village. In the 19th century CE, there were regular incursions: first by the French, under Napoleon Bonaparte, and then the British, under Horatio Nelson, who destroyed the French fleet and occupied Egypt.

The Ottoman sultan appointed Mohammed Ali, a Greek-born Albanian and distinguished soldier in the Turkish army, as governor of Alexandria and Egypt in 1805. Mohammed Ali saw the potential of the two ports and had the vision to bring British, French, Greeks and Jews to rebuild the city by offering them special privileges. As a result, in the late 19th and 20th century, modern Alexandria arose as a commercially-successful city with all types of industries, cultivating and exporting cotton, generating wealth and a good standard of living for everyone for 150 years.

In the 1950s, there was an explosion of Egyptian nationalism, a change to military rule and the closure of the Suez Canal, followed by the Anglo–French–Israeli invasion in 1956. The legacy of this military regime, under the leadership of Colonel Nasser, was the decline of Alexandria and the exodus of all its foreigners – including myself. I had the misfortune to witness these events, and realised that there was no future for any foreigner to live and work in Egypt. By 1962, some 85–90 percent had already left.

Efforts by Britain and the United States to stabilise Egypt failed, the Palestinian negotiations deteriorated, the rise of terrorist organisations was disturbing, the Arab countries' discontent with their leaders looked for solutions and, several decades later, the "Arab Spring" movement began. This book presents historical facts and information from the birth of geometry, astronomy, hydraulics, medicine and religious philosophy up until the beginnings of Christianity. Concerning modern Alexandria, it recounts the lives of a people with a European lifestyle – their economic, professional and social achievements – but the military revolution brought about the decline of the cosmopolitan city to an Arab summer resort.

It has taken several years to complete this book, but it was undoubtedly a "labour of love", as it is about my birthplace. I have deliberately kept it short, in the tradition of Kallimachos (the Alexandrian poet of the 3rd century BCE) who is quoted as saying "a big book is a difficult book!" Some changes were carried out with the spelling of proper names of people and places, differing from the usual Latinisation of Greek names and pronunciation that still prevails in the English-speaking world; however, I retained well-known and familiar names for the convenience of the reader.

All translations of ancient and modern Greek poetry and quotations are my own, unless otherwise stated. Instead of BC and AD I have used BCE (Before Christian Era) and CE (Christian Era) as this is now common practice.

Acknowledgements

I am grateful to my friends – scholars and experts in their own fields – for their interest and helpful suggestions. My special thanks go to Paul Cartledge; A. G. Leventis, professor of Greek culture, Clare College, University of Cambridge, England; Marion de Maisonneuve, archaeologist, USA; Patrick de Maisonneuve, professor of restorative architecture in Paris, France; Jeffery Carson, poet and teacher of creative writing at the Aegean Centre for Fine Arts in Paros, Greece; Curt Ebeling, Frankfurt, Germany (who shares my interest in underwater archaeological exploration in Alexandria); Stella Lubsen-Admiraal, archaeologist; Professor Jacobus Lubsen, cardiologist, Holland; Cynthia Cotts, journalist, New York; Gary Broadhurst, for his help with computer problems; the late Lambis Proukakis, professor of nuclear medicine and biographer, Athens, Greece; and Socrates Smyrnis, retired Greek Air Force squadron leader.

Peter Seibt, well-known artist working in Paros and Switzerland, designed the book cover, for which I hereby express my heartfel thanks. Christopher Stockdale, retired general practitioner and charity marathon swimmer, West Midlands, England, is gratefully acknowledged for his friendship and encouragement.

My sons, John and Jason, and stepson Kevin, deserve special thanks for their enthusiastic support and genuine interest in the history and my stories of Alexandria. I am indebted to my wife, Jean, who tirelessly typed the manuscript far too many times for corrections and additional material.

During the preparation of this book, a two-page extract

on "The Decline of Modern Cosmopolitan Alexandria" appeared in the *Anglo-Hellenic Review* (number 39, Spring 2009) – my thanks go to the editor, Paul Watkins.

I would like to express my gratitude to Anthony Grahame, Editorial Director at Sussex Academic, and his team, for their helpful collaboration in the publication process.

Books Consulted

The books consulted about the ancient city are numerous and those I found most helpful were E. M. Forster's *Alexandria: A History and a Guide*; P. M. Frazer's classic book on Ptolemaic Alexandria; and the published lectures from a symposium about the city held at the Getty Museum in Malibu, California, USA in 1996.

I read many books on science (presented in the Select Bibliography) including geometry, mathematics, mechanics and geography. Information about Alexander the Great, the founder of the city, is from two reliable sources. The first is the official source from Arrian (Arrianos) who used the diaries of Alexander's immediate entourage: Ptolemy Lagos, his general; Aristovoulos, the architect; Eumenes, his secretary; his official historian, Kallisthenes; and Nearchos, commander of Alexander's fleet. The second is the Vulgate source, which was written later but, nevertheless, adds to the historical events: from Kleitarchos, Diodorus Siculus, Curtius Quintus and Plutarch. From the modern historians, N. G. L. Hammond, Paul Cartledge and Paul Green have been the most helpful.

I have not used *The Alexander Romance* – a fictional book on his life during the Hellenistic period, spread throughout the centuries with all sorts of stories and myths. For modern Alexandria, where I witnessed events in the early 1950s – the military revolution, Suez Canal War, expulsion of the foreign communities and decline of the city to a provincial summer resort – my sources were the Egyptian, English, French and Greek newspapers and magazines of the time, local radio broadcasts, the *BBC World Service*, *Arab World Service* and biographies written by politicians and military officers. Of great use was George Antonius' book *Arab Awakening*, coincidentally written by the father of one of my school friends. I also used several American and British books concerning the strategy, diplomacy and economic policies of the United States, Great Britain and Egypt in 1880–1956.

Maps and Diagrams, with Narrative

The preliminary pages include three maps. The first depicts the eastern Mediterranean, Italy and Sicily. In the 2nd and 3rd centuries BCE, these were Greek colonies. Archimedes left Syracuse in Sicily to study in the Alexandrian Grand Library, as did Theokritos, the "pastoral poet", who went to live and write in the city. Macedonia, in the north of Greece, was the birthplace of Alexander the Great and Ptolemy I. Ionia, in Asia Minor, is on the east along the Aegean Sea, and further south is the Mediterranean Sea, Syria and Phoenicia. To the west of Egypt is Kyrene (present-day Libya) – a Ptolemaic colony, birthplace of Kallimachos the poet and Eratosthenes the mathematician. To the south is the city of Alexandria, on the shores of Egypt, west of the Nile delta.

The second map shows Alexander's military campaign route, starting from Macedonia, to Troy and then south, freeing the Greeks from the Persians in Ionia at the battles of Granicus and Issos. He then entered Egypt through Sinai, founded his city of Alexandria, and visited the Oracle of Amun in Siwa in the western desert. Here, he turned east towards Mesopotamia, to defeat Darius, the emperor of Persia, at the Battle of Gaugamela. After conquering the whole of Persia, he moved on to the Punjab, and then to India. After ten years of fighting, on his return home, he stopped in Babylon, where he died from an unknown cause in June 323 BCE.

The third map shows the empire of Ptolemy I, founder of the dynasty that lasted for three hundred years. His colonies were Kyrene on the west; the island of Cyprus, important for its copper mines; Syria, with its extensive territories and large population (in Hellenistic times, it was the Seleucid empire); and Phoenicia, the southern territory (present-day Lebanon).

The photograph on page 32 shows the Square of Saad Zaghloul on the coastal promenade – in 40 BCE, the site of Cleopatra's temple (alas, no archaeological remains are visible). Behind the tram terminal, the large building housed the British Irrigation Company where Cavafy the poet worked for thirty years in the early 1900s. On the ground floor is the Grand Trianon cafeteria, where I sat in my youth and from where I could imagine the ancient monuments of ancient Alexandria.

The map of modern Alexandria (page 34) contains street names and city buildings, with corresponding alerts to the sites of famed ancient buildings. This informative map will be of use to tourists and scholars when visiting the city.

The map of Ancient Alexandria's historical sites (page 70) was drawn by Mahmoud Bey al Falaki in 1865. I have superimposed labels indicating the important monuments of the 3rd century BCE: the lighthouse, palaces, Cleopatra's temple, the Grand Library and Museum, and, in the south-west, the Serapeion temple.

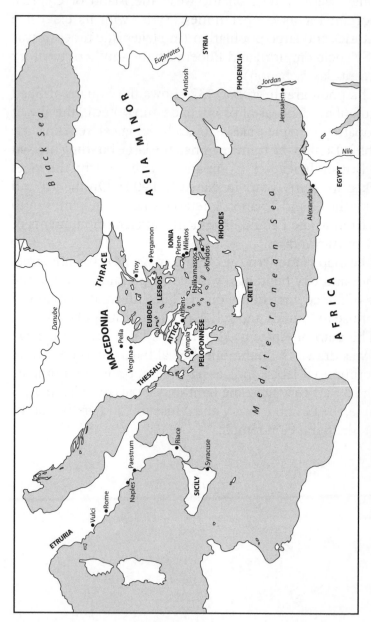

The Eastern Mediterranean, Italy, Sicily, Greece, Egypt and the Middle East, and key cities.

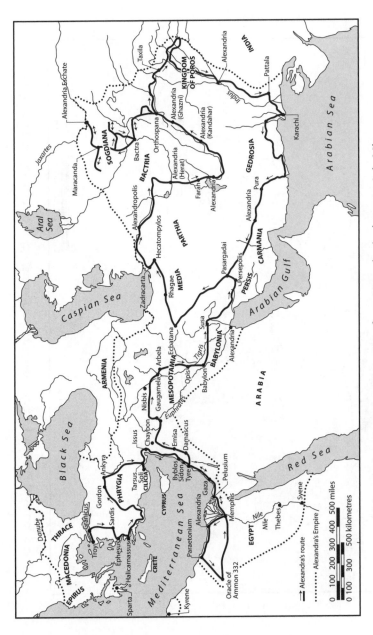

Alexander's conquering route map from Macedonia down to Asia Minor, Egypt, Persia and India.

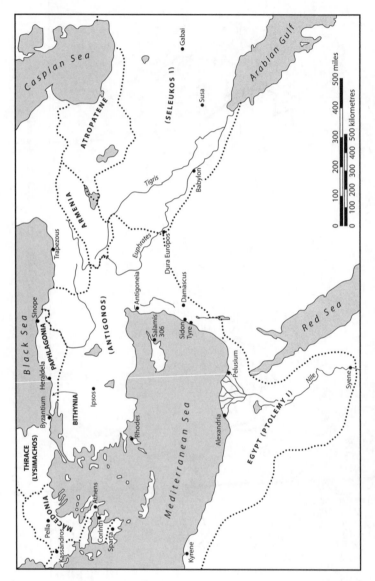

The colonies of Ptolemy I, from 320 to 303 BCE: Kyrene, Egypt, Salamis (Cyprus) and Syria.

Egypt is a *white pearl* in the months of July, August
and September, when it is immersed in water
and the villages built on hilltops look
like stars surrounded by a
shimmering white sea.

In October, November and December it
is dark musk when the waters recede,
leaving behind black soil.

It is like a green emerald in the months of January,
February and March, when the grasses and
plants shoot up out of the soil.

And a red gold in April May and June when the seeds
ripen and the grass takes on a golden hue, so
that it not only looks like gold but is
as bountiful as gold.

TENTH-CENTURY ARAB AUTHOR, AL-MASUDI

Introduction

Man is by nature a political animal.

Aristotle 384–322 BCE, *Politics*, book 1

The city of Alexandria in Egypt has two histories: in the 3rd century BCE, as the legendary ancient Greek centre of learning and, in the 19th and first half of the 20th century, as a commercially successful city with a European culture. At the start of the 21st century, Egypt is struggling to find political stability and rebuild its economy.

After the death of Alexander the Great, in 323 BCE, Ptolemy, son of Lagos, went to Egypt to start a dynasty and build the "illustrious city" on the chosen plot of land. The Macedonian Greeks constructed the first lighthouse, the Grand Library and Museum – that functioned as a university and was known as the "School of Alexandria" – and, with its successful port, it became the greatest emporium in the ancient world. Scholars from other countries, having heard of the reputation of the unique library in Alexandria, came to study, research, write and teach. Several "star scholars" appeared: Efklides (Euclid), the father of geometry; Archimedes, a true scientist; Aristarchos, who realised that the earth rotated around the sun; Claudios Ptolemy, the astronomer and geographer, and numerous other scientists. The western world has adopted and developed their discoveries throughout the centuries.

After three hundred years of Greek Ptolemaic rule, Alexandria was invaded by the Romans – an event that marked the start of the city's decline, and was accelerated by the beginnings of Christianity and sectarian conflicts.

This was followed by the rise of Islam and, in 645 CE, the Arab conquest, after which Alexandria was neglected – firstly by the Arabs, and then by the Turks. Finally, a series of natural disasters caused the collapse of the city.

The rebirth of Alexandria started in 1805 CE; the population of the city had dropped to a few thousand and there was a chronic lack of water, as the source from the west branch of the Nile had silted up. Mohammed Ali, the new viceroy, reopened the water supply by building a canal to ensure that there was water available at all times, in order that people could come to live and work in the city once again.

CHAPTER ONE is about Alexandria in the early 1950s, to set the scene for the readers to experience the European-style city in Egypt. When a country develops improved standards of education, the aspirations of its people change; thus it was to be expected that Egyptian nationalism would rise in reaction to the increasing number of foreigners living in their city and the British domination of Egypt since 1882. The "Free Officers" of the Egyptian army organised a bloodless revolution and, on 23 July 1952, abolished the monarchy and overthrew the government. This change to a military regime altered the behaviour of the Egyptians, who started to become militant and inward looking.

CHAPTER TWO is devoted to the poets and writers who spent some years living in Alexandria, and wrote poems and books making the city popular to the western world: Constantine Cavafy, the internationally-known Alexandrian poet, and Edward Morgan Forster and Laurence George Durrell, the renowned British writers. It includes short biographies with alluring stories, quotations of poetry and passages from their books.

CHAPTER THREE is entitled "Reflections on Ancient Alexandria: Replacing the Famed Monuments on their Rightful Sites". In modern Alexandria, it is incomprehensible that there is no visible evidence of three hundred years of the most successful ancient Greek city on the shores of Egypt. In Athens and Rome, the visitor can see evidence of those cities' former glory. This lack of any structure or building from the ancient city had a profound effect on me during my student days, and is reflected in the text.

Sitting in the city centre, facing the coast, my mind started to place the known ancient temples, palaces and monuments on their modern sites. The lighthouse, Grand Library, Museum, royal palaces, Cleopatra's temple, the Serapeion and the large marble-colonnaded avenues are set out in their rightful places. The square of Saad Zaghloul, facing the coastal promenade close to the tram terminus, is where Cleopatra's elegant temple once stood, while the Museum and Grand Library were on the southwest of the square, where most of today's high-rise apartments, cafeterias, restaurants and shops are built.

CHAPTER FOUR is a concise biography of Alexander, the founder of the city. It is essential to get to know the young military genius who, by the age of twenty-six, had liberated Asia Minor and Egypt, conquered Persia and travelled as far as India. Alexander had a unique education – his teacher was the great Aristotle who, along with other renowned scholars, introduced him to Athenian politics, democracy, ethics, literature, philosophy and science. People know Alexander mainly from books and films – often containing inaccurate history based on myths and gossip. He was an astute military strategist, diplomat, politician, visionary and city planner, who spread Hellenism to the East and improved the cultural lives of people in the conquered countries. Alexander's iconography, personal sculptors and painters are presented in some detail – their works were so impressive that they influenced western art throughout the centuries. There is also an interesting analysis of the possible cause of his death, with stories and conspiracy theories of the enemies who wanted him dead.

CHAPTER FIVE relates the quest for the elusive tomb of Alexander the Great. This is a special chapter, full of information set out in chronological order, and with many surprises! One can only imagine what would be the reaction of the world if his tomb were to be found – given the rapid dissemination of news, internet and social media, there probably would be more excitement than the finding of the tomb of Tutankhamun by Howard Carter in Egypt's Valley of the Kings in 1922.

CHAPTER SIX, entitled "Alexandria the Great", tells the story of how the city was built – the unique lighthouse, the Grand Library and Museum – the products of its scholars and inventors: thirteen books on geometry, a book on astronomy and geography, the *Almagest*, anatomical dissection that showed that the heart was a pump, and mechanical gadgets, such as a water pump, a system of pulleys, the first syringe, a water clock and a water musical organ that were all designed in ancient Alexandria.

CHAPTER SEVEN documents the collapse of ancient Alexandria. The causes are presented in historical order, starting with the accidental fire, the Roman invasion, the beginnings of Christianity, sectarian conflicts, the Arab invasion and natural disasters. The work of the team carrying out underwater archaeological research is fascinating, and is already starting to shed light upon the submerged monuments along the coast and further east.

CHAPTER EIGHT recounts the rebirth of Alexandria, which started in 1805 with the appointment of Mohammed Ali (an Albanian born in Greece and a successful soldier in the Turkish army) as governor and, later, viceroy of Egypt. The rebuilding of the city was achieved by encouraging Britons, Greeks, Jews and Italians to invest, work and live in Alexandria by offering them tax concessions and land for cultivation. It was their entrepreneurial efforts that made it the most prosperous Mediterranean city in which to live and work – until 1952.

CHAPTER NINE explains how the foreign communities played an important part in developing the European character of Alexandria, and how their most relevant contributions were to the field of education and the civic life of the city. There were good hospitals and institutions, religious freedom and mixed-tribunal courts for people to be tried and to appeal in their own language. The cosmopolitan stories are entertaining, as were the soldiers who were stationed with their families in Alexandria during the Second World War and during the Suez Canal War. Tourists who have spent time in the city and have read Forster or Durrell may recognise some of the British and Jewish personalities.

CHAPTER TEN, entitled "Four Years of Uncertainty and Anxiety: 1952–1956", presents the dramatic events as the political changes unfolded. This and the subsequent chapters are unique, because the author was an eyewitness to the political changes that were taking place at that time. The political mistake of Egypt's leader, Gamal Abdel Nasser, was to act in anger and nationalise the Suez Canal (the property of an Anglo-French company) in 1956, without considering the consequences of how such an action could lead to a war.

CHAPTER ELEVEN, "The Suez Canal War", discusses how the Anglo–French–Israeli invasion was triggered by the closure and nationalisation of the Suez Canal by Egypt's military regime; the war that followed (known as the "Eden-Mollet folly") produced worldwide condemnation, international commercial havoc and accusations that the western leaders could not find a workable solution with the Egyptian leaders. The effects of this war were felt for a long time in Europe, particularly by every family in Britain, because of the subsequent petrol shortage and rationing. Nasser's other mistake was the vengeful expropriation of all foreign assets in the name of socialism, which resulted in the exodus of the foreign residents. This created domestic problems in Egypt, with increased unemployment, a decline in cotton exports and no foreign investment.

CHAPTER TWELVE considers the reasons for the decline of modern Alexandria. These are numerous, starting with a dysfunctional monarchy, incompetent politicians, over-zealous Egyptian nationalism and, sadly, the inability of western leaders to understand the needs of the educated generation of Egyptians – the legacy of this is the "Arab Spring".

The title of the book is partly allegorical. *The City of Gifts* is ancient Alexandria, which initiated and opened science to the western mind. Its scholars' work – inventing geometry and mechanics, realising the benefits of the steam engine, drawing a fairly accurate map of the world and the discovery of longitude and latitude – are some of its gifts.

The City of Sorrows is modern Alexandria: a successful multi-ethnic city through trade and cotton cultivation, with British, Greeks, Jewish and Egyptians living in harmony for 150 years. Its sorrows came with the unexpected revolution by the Egyptian military in 1952, the closure of the Suez Canal that was followed by the war, and the expulsion of all foreign communities, which brought unemployment, poverty and decline to the city.

CHAPTER ONE

Alexandria in the Early 1950s
The Beginning of the End

After the Second World War, political unrest was a serious problem in Alexandria. The young generation of better-educated Egyptians developed an interest in party politics and, very soon afterwards, there was a worrying increase in nationalism and the growth of a secret fundamentalist organisation: the Muslim Brotherhood. The request by the Egyptian authorities to dismantle the British military bases was a constant topic of discussion and, by 1951, Anglo-Egyptian negotiations were failing, while sabotage was being operated against British camps in Alexandria and the Suez Canal zone.

The following year, there was an escalation of clashes between British troops and the Egyptian police. There was genuine concern about these events by the United States, which tried to resolve the Anglo-Egyptian dispute by negotiating with the British and Egyptians to find a mutually beneficial political solution. Demonstrations in Cairo and Alexandria became frequent and violent; on 26 January 1952 ("Black Saturday"), the nationalists, together with the Muslim Brotherhood, burnt down buildings.

The breakaway "Free Officers" group of the Egyptian Army, whose strength and determination had been underestimated by the king, the government, the British and the secret services, suddenly gained considerable power and popularity, culminating in a bloodless military coup on 23 July 1952.

The revolutionary forces occupied the royal palace and overthrew the government. On 26 July 1952, the head of the military regime, General Mohammed Naguib, went to the Pharos peninsula in Alexandria to ask King Farouk, who was spending his summer holidays in his palace, to sign the prepared abdication papers. The king offered no resistance, fearing for his own life and the lives of his family. When the official documents were completed, the family boarded the royal yacht *Mahrousa* to journey into exile in Italy, the king's choice. General Naguib bid them a formal farewell and, after a twenty-one-gun salute at 6:00 p.m., they sailed away on the same boat that had been used to depose a previous ruler (Khedive Ismail) in 1875, for mismanaging the economy.

One would have thought that, after these terrifying revolutionary events, people would panic – especially the foreigners – but this did not happen. We had been expecting change, but this happened so fast (within forty-eight hours) that there was no time to take in the long-term consequences. King Farouk had been unpopular for years, and the British army had overstayed their welcome in Egypt. My parents were not alarmed, and my generation remained unaffected for a time, as we looked somewhat favourably at the leaders of the "Free Officers" who had led a revolution without bloodshed. Etched in my memory is a warm September evening in 1953, fourteen months after the revolution, walking along the coastal promenade from home in Laurens, an eastern suburb, to meet friends in the city centre. We had arranged to have a snack before going to the cinema, which was showing a *Twentieth Century Fox* film, "The Robe": a pseudo-biblical epic, and the first cinemascope movie to be shown in Alexandria. Hollywood made such themes spectacular and entertaining – very different from the Egyptian and European films of the time that generally dealt with social realism.

It was enjoyable walking during the early evening; the

promenade was less crowded than the year before, and one could lean on the iron railings and watch the colour changes in the sky and the sea at sunset. Just before reaching the city centre, by the eastern harbour, there is a promontory named Silselah that, in ancient times, was a large peninsula named Cape Lochias, where the Ptolemies built their palaces. After two tsunamis, the entrance to the eastern harbour (the "Gate of the Moon") and the boundary wall subsided into the sea.

The place where we were going to meet, Ramleh Station (the electric tram terminal), was always busy with people coming and going – an important focal point of the city. The tram was, and still is, the most popular and convenient form of transportation from the city centre to various districts, to the south and west, the eastern suburbs and their beach resorts. The tram system in Alexandria is one of the oldest in the world, with the main line running parallel to the coast. The tram consists of a double-decker coach for second-class passengers, attached to a single-decker coach for first class. It starts in the city centre at Ramleh ("sand" in Arabic) and ends in the east, in the suburb of Siouf, at Victoria station – so named as it was situated at the rear of the English public school, Victoria College. In 1914, Lord Meath, the representative of the British government, paid the school a visit and was impressed, calling it "the Eton of the Middle East" and lauding its tradition of character building.

All around the tram terminus were the cinemas, theatres, restaurants, patisseries and cafeterias. By the coastline, there is a square with a bronze statue of nationalist leader Saad Zaghloul, who started a nationalistic revolution and expressed anti-British sentiments, so the authorities exiled him to the Seychelles in 1919.

On the left of the square, by the coastline, is the Cecil Hotel – a favourite for many because of its extensive views and its art nouveau décor. Its "Monty Piano Bar" was named after General Montgomery, who spent some days in Alexandria planning the battle of El Alamein that took place in November 1942 and defeated Field-Marshal Erwin Rommel (the "Desert Fox"), preventing the German Nazis from occupying Egypt and moving on to the Suez Canal.

Along the coastal promenade, popularly known as the Corniche, there are several chic café-bar restaurants, including the Grand Trianon and Athineos (with an art décor interior) and, further along to the east, dinner-and-dance restaurants and nightclubs. In most streets around the tram terminus, there were traditional Greek patisseries, but the most popular for the European community was Delice, known for its exquisite cakes. In the other direction was the Elite cafe-bar and restaurant, with an extension across a broad pavement facing three cinemas – a meeting place mostly for foreigners, who were often entertained by the waiter Stelios Koumoutsos, an interesting amateur archaeologist with obsessive but passionate ideas as to the whereabouts of the tomb of Alexander the Great. He carried out many unofficial digs at several sites but, unfortunately, nothing was found, and he left for Greece, disappointed, in 1960. Those who knew him were saddened because there was no one else so interested and eager to find something from the Ptolemaic period.

An important and attractive landmark was, and still is, the square of Mohammed Ali, the founder of the modern city who encouraged foreign businessmen to live and work with Egyptians. As one entered the square, on the right of the statue, were the mixed tribunals where foreigners could be tried in their own language – a great concession by the authorities. On the left were the French Gardens stretching to the New Quays, a fine promenade from the south of Quait Bay along the coast of the eastern harbour to Silselah. The land on the north of the square was given as a gift to the British to construct the Anglican Church of Saint Mark. At the end of the square was the Bourse (the cotton and stock exchange) – an arcaded building with a large clock, and the most important trading centre in the country. The Bourse was burnt down in 1977, by reactionary nationalists aiming to remove European institutions from Egypt.

The street leading from the left of the square was Cherif Street, with its numerous chic boutiques and attractive buildings similar to Bond Street in London. The end of Cherif Street opened into Tousoum Street, dominated by an attractive Italianate building (the Bank of Rome) designed by British architect Henry Gorra, who was also responsible for designing Victoria College.

Behind the Cinema Amir, which mainly showed Hollywood films, was the internationally-known Pastroudis café with its white exterior and relief panels of columns, and a white entrance with contrasting awning. The interior was art nouveau, very atmospheric, and had excellent service, the waiters wearing white jackets and dark trousers – a Parisian-style cafeteria. It was here that the English writer Lawrence Durrell met Eve Cohen, who became his second wife and upon whom he based the first book of his *Alexandrian Quartet* – "Justine". Pastroudis was considered to be the favourite meeting place for foreign artists, poets and writers.

A newcomer, Elizabeth Gwynne (who later changed her name to Elizabeth David), joined the group. She had left England for Paris to study art, but was trapped by the Nazi invasion of France, escaped and went to Alexandria, where she worked for the British government during the Second World War. Whilst living in the city, she had a cook who was the inspiration for her Mediterranean-style cuisine. She was impressed with the fresh produce and cooking styles of France, Greece and Alexandria, and wrote her popular *Book of Mediterranean Cuisine* on her return to England, which was published by Lehman in 1950. A change to the taste buds of the British is attributed to this book that introduced herbs, olive oil and spices into everyday cooking.

After the Second World War, the population of the foreign communities in Alexandria was 240,000, including 110,000 Greeks. Before, and after, the First and Second World Wars, up until 1952, Alexandria thrived commercially and socially with a multi-ethnic community. Exiled royal families from the Balkans, Albania, Bulgaria, Greece, Italy and Yugoslavia all sought refuge, and brought with them their relatives and entourages, as King Farouk offered these exiled families generous and extended hospitality.

There were visits to Alexandria by the opera company Teatro de la Scala di Milano, Comedie Francaise, the Greek National Theatre, British orchestras and the Vienna Philharmonic, while Russian and French ballet companies also performed regularly.

One Friday evening, we had arranged to go to Aiglon, a dinner-and-dance restaurant that faced the coastal esplanade, close to the tram terminus. In our group were Egyptians, Greeks, Lebanese and Copts, but nearly all of our British and Jewish friends had already left Egypt. We missed them, remembering the good times we had had together at parties and the summer weekends on the beaches. The ballroom was beautifully arranged, with flowers on every table; the Egyptian waiters wore brown *galabeyas* (long robes) embroidered with gold thread and the Greek waiters wore white tuxedos. To our surprise, from the wings of the stage emerged musicians wearing Latin American clothing and large hats, pushing two harps on wheels while the rest of them held guitars. They were announced as "the famous Latin American band, Los Paraguayos" – this could only happen in cosmopolitan Alexandria! We had a memorable evening, with exhilarating and romantic music, hoping that the night would never end.

Alexandria had several municipal gardens along the Mahmoudieh Canal, which drew water from the west branch of the Nile; the smallest of them was the French

Gardens, on the northern part of Mohammed Ali Square. This lush green strip stretched at right angles to the New Quays.

Khedive Ismail, grandson of Mohammed Ali, established the Nouzha public gardens near a densely-populated suburb called Cleopatra, although the Ptolemaic queen never lived there. During the 3rd and 2nd centuries BCE, the area surrounding Nouzha was called Eleusis and was where Kallimachos the poet lived. These gardens consisted of approximately eight acres of tropical vegetation with old, well-maintained trees, and large grassy areas and shelters where families could picnic and watch their children play. During the First World War, this was the favourite garden of the English writer E. M. Forster, who enjoyed walking there during the evenings.

Looking at an old family album, I saw two photographs of my father taking me for a walk in the Nouzha Gardens, at the age of two, with reins around my waist and shoulders so I could not run off and explore. There were donkey rides, a zoological garden and, on Thursday and Sunday afternoons, a brass band would play on the ornate bandstand.

At the far end, there was a pelican pond and a gate that led into another very large garden, donated by Antony Antoniades, containing impressive limestone and marble statues dotted around. This forty-acre park had in its centre a large column of Aswan granite. It was dense with trees and tropical flowers all year round, and was as equally popular as the Corniche and beaches, particularly during the days of autumn and spring.

The Antoniades Garden extended into the suburb of Smouha Garden City, known for its tennis club, golf course and a very popular horse-riding school, run by a retired Englishman who had worked at the royal stables in Britain and came to live in Egypt after the death of George VI. At the back of several schools in Chatby district were the well-tended Shallalat Gardens, with interesting small waterfalls and large shady areas particularly appealing in the summer months.

The Alexandrian Corniche – the pride of the city and frequently compared to the French Riviera – is a twelve-mile (twenty-kilometre) coastal promenade with a wide walking area. It starts in the west, at the Fort of Kait Bey on the Pharos peninsula, where the ancient lighthouse had stood for more than a thousand years. All along the coast, from west to east, were numerous summer resorts with fine sandy beaches and excellent bathing facilities: wooden cabins, located on three tiers of promenades, for resting and changing into bathing suits, each with its own veranda and separated from the adjacent cabins by cloth dividers; overhead, a long cloth awning was fastened to the parapet to provide shade.

Interspersed between the resorts were restaurants and bars called "casinos" – not for gambling, but for dinner and dance. In the east, the Corniche ended at Montazah, an eighteen-square-mile   (twenty-four-square-kilometre) wooded area with sandy beaches and pretty gardens, which was the main summer palace of the Egyptian rulers before the military revolution. The architecture of the palace was a mixture of Moorish, Ottoman and Florentine styles, built by Khedive Abbas Helmi II and later renovated by Egypt's first king, Fuad I.

Everyone who lived close to the coast, as well as those from the suburbs, came to walk along the promenade with their families in the evenings, to enjoy the view and feel refreshed by the cool breeze during the hot summer months. Alexandria was, and still is, the summer capital of Egypt – during the early 1950s, there were almost one million summer visitors spending their holidays away from the stifling heat of Cairo and Upper Egypt. Alexandria, with its cooling northerly winds, beautiful beaches, gardens and varied entertainment, was ideal for family holidays. Parts of the promenade were teeming with peddlers pushing their handcarts and selling soft drinks, charcoal-grilled corn on the cob, lupine seeds and bread rolls with sesame seeds.

Along the broad pavement, romantic, leather-hooded, horse-drawn carriages were parked waiting for people to take a trip along the Corniche or around the city. Before cars came to Alexandria, apart from the trams, these carriages were the only form of transportation.

During the summer, it was especially pleasant to walk along the Corniche in the month of Ramadan. Ramadan occurs during the ninth month of the Muslim year, and believers must fast for up to fourteen hours (from sunrise to sunset), waiting for the gunshot sound that marks the end of the day's fast – at night, there was always a festive atmosphere. As a student, I would join the fast with my friends, and realised how difficult it was to go without water and food for so many hours each long, hot day – for a month.

A quotation from Byron's poem *Childe Harold's Pilgrimage* (Canto II, verse LX) is about Ramadan. Byron captures the essence of the fasting very well, but calls it *Ramazani*, preferring to use the Greek pronunciation as he was fluent in that language:

Just at this season Ramazani's fast,
Through the long day its penance did maintain:
But when the lingering twilight hour was past,
Revand feast assumed the rule again.

The internationally-known Egyptian singer Om Khalsoum, "the nightingale of the Arab world", would broadcast a concert on the radio once a month, on a Thursday evening, and everyone tuned in to hear her exceptional voice and the sheer strength of her performance that elevated social and love songs to the level of classical verse. These hot summer nights were sensual: the shutters of the houses closed, music from the radio, the aroma of

Egyptian food in the air and the anticipation of pleasures to come.

In the early 1950s, most people who walked on the Corniche in the evening were from the foreign communities or Egyptians who wore European clothes – only a few wore traditional Arab robes. Of those who did, the men wore the *galabeya*: white or coloured long, loose garments down to the ankles, with a round neck, while women wore the *melayah*: a black wrap-around garment over a dress, down to the ankle, which covered the head but left the face uncovered. When tied around the body, this accentuated the female body's contours. These loose garments were useful in the long, hot summers and kept the body cool. They were also practical to lift easily, in order to wash the feet before entering the mosque for prayers. Yet long robes were a significant symbol, and every time someone donned one, male or female, it was perceived as a kind of gesture to reclaim the city's status – or perhaps to cover up a secret.

After the Egyptian military coup in 1952, there were very few Europeans, but many more Egyptians with their traditional dress – a sign of nationalism. Those changes may have been worrying for the foreign communities but, on the other hand, we thought that it may have been a good thing for the Alexandrians to find their own identity while allowing a certain amount of multi-ethnic influence upon the fields of education, technology and international business management. For example, London, Paris and New York developed into international capitals and business centres, with hundreds of nationalities and creeds all working together to provide good education, institutions, research centres, good medical services and industries. If Alexandria had retained some of its entrepreneurial foreigners, it may have developed into a leading Mediterranean city and port.

CHAPTER TWO

Poets and Writers in Alexandria

There were three internationally known writers who made Alexandria popular to the contemporary world, with their poetry and books describing the lifestyle of the city in its cosmopolitan heyday.

Constantine Cavafy

A Greek gentleman in a straw hat standing absolutely motionless at a slight angle to the universe.
E. M. Forster

For the Greeks, the English-speaking world and Europeans, modern Alexandria would have been an orphan without Constantine Cavafy, who became "the soul and intellectual father of the city" and one of the greatest poets of the 20th century. His poetry was introduced to the English-speaking world by E. M. Forster, W. H. Auden and Rae Dalvin. Edmund Keeley and Philip Sherrard translated his poems, and they are now part of English literature – making Cavafy an internationally-esteemed poet. His poetry covers many themes – historical, personal, about Alexandria and erotic – and are usually short, full of expression, laden with irony and easily recognisable as Cavafy's poetry. They are written in "demotic" (the simplified language based on popular speech) interspersed with "katharevousa" (a purer form of the language). His poetry is characterised by the synthesis of the past and present that gave to the city a new mythology.

Cavafy started publishing poems in 1884, at the age of twenty-one, in periodicals, pamphlets and broadsheets, and distributed them to his friends. Later, he insisted that his poems should be divided into those written before and after 1911. His total output of poems was around 245, of which seventy-five were unpublished at the time of his death. He wrote approximately seventy poems a year, of which he kept four or five and destroyed the rest. Contemporary puritanical values made it socially unacceptable, because of his homosexuality, for his poems to be read in schools or universities in Alexandria or Athens. My parents neither discussed Cavafy at home during my adolescence, nor with the people who visited us and who had stories to tell about his life and his poetry.

The Alexandrian Greeks, poor or rich, were surprisingly Victorian in their attitudes. Cavafy neither referred to his homosexuality nor breeched the limits of decency of that period. In 1901, Peter Anastasiades, a close friend educated in England, anxious that Cavafy's work should be recognised in Greece, paid his expenses for a literary tour to Athens to meet editors and poets. On his second trip, in 1903, Cavafy met the well-known writer Xenopoulos, who selected twelve of his poems and published them in an Athenian magazine, while the popular poet Costas Ouranis, who called Alexandria "the seat of Greek literature", was the first poet to publicly praise Cavafy.

Despite such support, most of the Athenian literati kept their distance and did not acknowledge him for a long time, until Forster, Durrell, Seferis (the 1963 Nobel laureate) and W. H. Auden started writing complimentary reviews.

Constantine Cavafy was born in Alexandria on 29 April 1863, the youngest of nine children. His father, Peter John, was a prominent cotton merchant from a well-to-do family, and was one of the first Alexandrians to work together with the British to start a cotton-ginning factory to mechanically remove the cotton from the seed – at the time, considered to be pioneering work. His mother, Hariclea, was very devoted to her children; when she lost her only daughter, Eleni, she was inconsolable. Constantine was her youngest child and, to compensate for the loss of her daughter, she dressed him like a girl, leaving his hair to grow long and curly. Hariclea was the eldest daughter of a diamond merchant in Constantinople, Istanbul, whose family came from Chios in the 1700s. Peter John died in 1870, when Constantine was seven years old, leaving the family with little money.

They had always lived in an expensive area, provided a meeting place for the wealthy Alexandrian society, entertained frequently, spent their holidays in England, France and Italy, and must have lived beyond their means. Two years later, the mother took the children to England, where the eldest son was managing a cotton business in London and Liverpool. They stayed in England for five years; two of the brothers went to a private school but Constantine was tutored at home.

He was an avid reader, interested in Latin, history and French. English became his second language, and he spoke the language with an upper-class accent. His relationship with other boys was casual – he did not make close friends or play sports, nor was he interested in pretty English girls. Surprisingly, he enjoyed adult gatherings at parties and invitations to afternoon tea, always appearing serious as a way to disguise his shyness.

When the family returned to Alexandria in 1879, he continued his education at a private school. Three years later, there was a nationalist uprising organised by a minister, Ahmed al Orabi, which turned into a religious revolt rather than a political demonstration. The crisis worsened, and there were cries in the streets of "kill Christians", resulting in many deaths. The British did not react immediately, and twenty thousand foreigners left Alexandria. Mrs Cavafy had no choice but to take her sons to Istanbul, where they stayed at the house of her eighty-year-old father for three years.

This was an eventful period in the private life of Constantine – it was in the streets, clubs and *hammams* (baths) of Istanbul that he was introduced to homosexuality. After his return to Alexandria, he frequented brothels and billiard rooms in Messala, where he met young men. His early poems do not reveal any homoeroticism but, in his fifties, he started to express those feelings.

The "Greek kings of Cotton" (Choremi and Benaki) offered Cavafy jobs but he refused them, contemplating a career in journalism – which did not materialise. Eventually, he went to work as a clerk at the British Department of Irrigation, where he remained fully employed for thirty years, with a good salary, security and plenty of time to read and write his poems.

In 1907, he moved to the second floor of a house: 10 Rue Lepsius (recently renamed Sharm el Sheikh Street). On the ground floor was a brothel, where the "girls" were very respectful to the poet, and he used to say to his visitors: "Poor things, one must feel sorry for them." Opposite his apartment was the old Greek hospital, Saint Sofronios, where the bacteriologist Robert Koch (who was in Alexandria in the late 1880s, during a short-lived epidemic of cholera) had identified the comma-shaped bacillus. On the other side of the street stands the Church of Saint Savas, which was, until recently, the offices of the Patriarchate, but has now moved into the grounds of the Greek Church of the Annunciation Virgin Mary in Attarine. In his home, Cavafy would receive friends and visitors, preferring to sit in the dark, close to the window, smoking, talking and gesticulating while his manservant offered whisky, liqueurs and a large variety of snacks.

In 1932, Cavafy was diagnosed with cancer of the throat and went to Athens for treatment. The growth increased, and surgeons carried out a tracheotomy to help him breathe, but he lost his speech. He kept by his side a notepad, so that he could communicate with friends and also write poetry. A few days before he died, he asked a family friend, Rika Singopoulos, to find a reference that he needed to complete a historical poem – he was meticulous up to the very end of his life. He was fortunate to have support from the Singopoulos couple, who not only nursed him but also kept his manuscripts, articles, journals and newspapers, which have proved helpful to his biographers. Constantine Cavafy died on his birthday, 29 April 1933, in the Greek hospital; the Patriarch Meletios gave him the final rites. He is buried in the Greek cemetery in Chatby, in a marble tomb two rows away from where my parents are buried.

A quotation from one of his personal poems, *The Walls* (published in 1896), expresses his loneliness – and maybe his guilt concerning his sexuality:

Without prudence, without sorrow, without modesty,
Thick and high walls have been built around me.
And I sit here now in despair
I think of nothing else, my mind is consumed by this fate
Outside I have a lot of things to do.
When they were erecting the walls why was I not more careful
I never heard any building noises or any sound
Unnoticeably they closed me in from the outside world.

The City, written in 1910, is about Alexandria, where he spent all his adult life but often was unhappy. However, if anyone suggested he should move to Athens, he refused, as Alexandria was his "muse":

You said "I will go to another land, cross another sea
Another city I will find better than this."
Every effort of mine is destined to fail
And my heart is seemingly dead – buried.
How long will my mind continue to pine away

Wherever I turn my eye, wherever I gaze,
Dark ruins of my life are visible.
I have wasted and destroyed so many years.

In the Tavernas, a erotic poem with a historical angle, published in 1926, and translated by Edmund Keeley and Philip Sherrard:

I wallow in the tavernas and brothels of Beirut.
I did not want to stay
in Alexandria. Tamides left me;
He went off with the Prefect's son and earned himself
a villa on the Nile, a mansion in the city.
It wouldn't have been decent for me to stay in Alexandria.
I wallow in the tavernas and brothels of Beirut.
I live a vile life devoted to cheap debauchery.
The one thing that saves me,
like durable duty, like perfume
that goes on clinging to my flesh is this:
Tamides, most exquisite of young men, was mine for two years,
mine completely and not because of a house or a villa on the Nile.

Cavafy had been interested in history since adolescence, and wrote 154 historical poems.

Theophilos Paleologos, published in 1914, relates the fate of the Greek people, translated by Edmund Keeley and Philip Sherrard:

His is the last year, and the last
Of the Greek emperors. And, alas,
How sadly those around me talk.
Kyr Theophilos Paleologos
In his grief, and despair, said:
"I would rather die than live".
Ah, Kyr Theophilos Paleologos
How much pathos, the yearning of our race,

How much weariness –
Such exhaustion from injustice and persecution
Your six tragic words contained.
[The word *Kyr* is shortened from *Kyrie*, which in Greek
means "Lord".]

Cavafy's poem, *Ithaka*, published in 1910, was chosen by
Jackie Kennedy-Onassis to be read at her funeral service.
To bring it to life, it is worth quoting the first three lines,
translated by Edmund Keeley and Philip Sherrard:

"As you set out for Ithaka
Hope the road is a long one,
Full of adventure, full of discovery."

Another two widely-read poems are *Waiting for the
Barbarians* and *The God Abandons Antony*. In these last
poems, he fuses myth and reality, the past and the present
and, more importantly, the poet and the hero. They are
quoted extensively in modern English literature, and this is
why I have chosen his lesser-known poems to represent
each of the categories. It was not until thirty years after his
death that he gained recognition as a major poet in the
English-speaking world, and his poems have now been
translated into many European languages.

The Greek biographers have fallen short in presenting
the complete life of Cavafy. Timos Malanos (1935) is only
partially biographical; Michael Perides (1948) is sketchy;
and Stratis Tsirkas (1958) published a social and political
analysis rather than a scrutiny of his personal life and
poetry. The only real biographer of Cavafy was the
Englishman Robert Liddell, who published his book in
1974, but leaves some gaps in Cavafy's life when in England
and in his late-twenties in Alexandria. However, Edmund
Keeley's *Cavafy's Alexandria* (1976) is a superb "guide" to
his poems.

What is really needed is a new biography of Cavafy's personal life from manuscripts, letters, unpublished work, archives that have been previously unavailable to the public, the right kind of gossip and a proper literary assessment of his poetry.

In 1991, I went to Egypt at the invitation of the Egyptian military to demonstrate new operative techniques at two hospitals in Cairo. A few days later, an opportunity arose to visit Alexandria with my wife and some friends so, with great excitement, we went first to Cavafy's apartment and afterwards to his library. We were disappointed and deflated that there were no other visitors and that the attendants in both places were unhelpful.

We were told that few people visit this apartment on Sharm el Sheikh Street or his library, housed in the Greek consulate (previously the Greek Community High School) in the district of Chatby. Most of the Egyptians, and the few remaining Greeks in Alexandria, sadly, have no interest in one of the greatest poets of our time.

To recover from this disappointing visit, we walked along the coastal promenade to take deep breaths and to reflect that, paradoxically, Cavafy's popularity as a poet in the West is on the increase while, in Alexandria – where he was born, worked and wrote his poetry – he is forgotten.

Edward M. Forster

The great English author who wrote the very best
guidebook to Alexandria

Edward Morgan Forster went to Alexandria as a conscientious objector in November 1915, during the First World War, with the intention of helping the Red Cross in Egypt. He was born in London in 1879, studied at King's College, Cambridge and, by the time he arrived in Alexandria, he was already an acclaimed author following the success of his books *Where Angels Fear to Tread, The Longest Journey, A Room with a View* and *Howards End*. Forster got to know Alexandria very well, travelling on foot and by tram, either on his own or accompanied by a young Egyptian tram conductor who became his close friend.

He started writing *Alexandria: A History and a Guide* during the first year. It took him four years to complete but did not reach the public until 1922, due to publishing problems. It is a unique guide to the city, containing scholarly information and written in stimulating style. Forster's room-to-room description of the Greco-Roman Museum is meticulous, revealing both his deep interest in history and his knowledge of archaeology.

His chapter on modern Alexandria in the early 1900s is presented in eight sections, going from one landmark to another, making the reader feel that he is accompanying Forster on his walks – in fact, he describes some areas that even those who have lived all their life in Alexandria have never visited.

An astute observation by Forster in his guide book is that Alexandria was on the edge of western civilisation, with the desert to the south. It is often forgotten that the desert had played an important role in preserving early Christianity, as the monasteries and churches were used as sanctuaries to keep Christians safe from pagans and, later, from invading Arabs.

His stay in Alexandria was of immense importance to the literary world – he was introduced to Cavafy by a Cambridge friend, Robert Furness. Forster read and enjoyed the translated poems and, in his second book, *Pharos and Pharillon*, presented Cavafy and introduced his poetry to his English-speaking readers.

Whilst at Cambridge, he had been a member of the Apostles Society (formally the Cambridge Conversazione society), and many of its members later became the core of the Bloomsbury Group. His friends Leonard and Virginia

Woolf helped Forster with his typesetting and rushed the second edition, published by Hogarth Press. It was meant as a novelist's sketchbook of Alexandria through the ages. Forster, in *Alexandria: A History and a Guide*, approaches the sites of the city as a tourist guide linking the past and the present.

When Forster returned to England in 1919, he wrote to George Savides, the poet's friend and publisher, saying that "meeting Cavafy and talking about his poetry was one of the highlights of my life". Maybe Forster also felt guilty about his homosexuality but, in Alexandria, he was able to pursue his relationship with his friend Mohammed al Adl without malicious gossip.

Forster must have looked back on his interesting and happy times in Alexandria, remembering the friends he had made, the walks he so enjoyed both in the city and by the coast – usually with excellent weather – and it was reported that he "bathed naked in the sea like Cleopatra".

Forster was angered because of increasing nationalistic attacks on British and Europeans due to the prolonged British domination, with cries in the streets of "Egypt for the Egyptians", and he wrote letters expressing his views to the *Manchester Guardian* (in March 1919) and the *Daily Herald* (in May of the same year), disapproving of British colonialism, attacking British policy in Egypt and the callous treatment of the *fellahine* (farmers).

This influenced the British High Commissioner for Egypt to take action and, some time later, the British government gave the country partial sovereignty – but it took until the 1950s for the British troops to leave.

Lawrence G. Durrell

*"The Alexandrian Quartet", cosmopolitan multi-love stories
that made him world famous*

Lawrence George Durrell, English author and poet, spent his childhood in India and his adolescence in Corfu, Greece. When he returned to spend time on the island, he corresponded with Henry Miller, the New York author who had just published his book *Tropic of Cancer* that impressed Durrell so much, he invited Miller to travel to Greece to get to know each other and to enjoy the country.

Before the Second World War, Durrell had met George Katsimbalis, a writer interested in contemporary Greek literature who had launched a self-funded literary journal named *Ta Nea Grammata* (The New Letters) that published the poems of Seferis and Elytis (who both became Nobel poet laureates, in 1963 and 1979, respectively). He also edited the annual *Anglo-Hellenic Review* that published the works of British and Greek writers. Another publication was *Modern Greek Poets*, which consisted of poems by Kostis Palamas and Theodore Stephanides (a physician and poet, whom Miller described as "the most learned man he ever met"), but only one poem by Cavafy.

When Henry Miller came to Athens, Durrell introduced him to his group of friends, – Katsimbalis, Seferis and Nikos Ghikas (a great Greek painter in the class of Picasso), and together they had regular gatherings in Athens and travelled to various parts of Greece.

While in Greece, Miller wrote a wonderful book, *The Colossus of Maroussi*, about his journey to Greece, the peace and joy he found there, and the intellectual stimulation and friendship within his group – particularly with Katsimbalis, the eponymous "Colossus" upon whom he based the story.

Lawrence Durrell had fled from Greece during the Second World War, just before the Nazi occupation. He was given a job at the British embassy in Cairo and, two years later, moved to Alexandria as a press officer in the British Information Office. He worked in the city centre, on the first floor of a building a few metres' walk from Cherif Street that joins the main thoroughfare, El Horreya, where my father worked for an English company.

Nearby is the Mohammed Ali Club, a meeting place for Egyptian politicians, European writers and celebrities. On the corner was Maison Baudrot, a very fashionable patisserie and restaurant, where stories circulated that Madame Baudrot bathed in milk, smoked cigars and, some nights, wore only white furs on her naked body – tales that surely stirred up ideas for Durrell's books.

From letters to his friends, it seems that Alexandria had no appeal for him, as Durrell had always been inspired by Greece, and most of his books were about the islands and their people; yet, the book that made him world famous was about Alexandria! In 1945, after the liberation of Greece, he left Egypt and went to live with his second wife, Eve Cohen, and their daughter. After their later separation, he moved to Cyprus, bought a house and taught English literature at a school – and it was there that he met Claude-Marie Vincendon, the granddaughter of Baron Felix de Menasce, Alexandrian cotton merchant and banker. It is said that she "fell into his arms", inspiring him instantly to start writing *The Alexandrian Quartet*, which was completed after moving to France. The book became an instant critical and commercial success in the English-speaking world.

I remember that, during an interview for an orthopaedic training post in England in 1963, I was asked by a member of the interview committee if I had read *The Alexandria Quartet*. My reply was that I had, and had enormously enjoyed Durrell's prose, twice reading some passages from "Justine", the first book, which had impressed me. However, I said that I did not feel he had captured the real Alexandria, with the abject poverty of the Egyptians, the rise of nationalism, the general unrest and the uncertainty of the foreign communities about their future. I sensed that my interviewer was displeased with my opinion but, nevertheless, he offered me the post and we got on very well.

Durrell, with his poetic prose picturing Alexandria through sounds and smells: "the clang of the trams shuddering in their metal veins", the "sweet smell of brick dust and the odour of pavements slaked with water" and the atmosphere like that of a painting: "dust red, dust green, chalk mauve", was sheer poetry. He portrayed the lifestyle of the foreign elite as decadent, although the majority of them were actually Victorian in their attitudes, but he glamorised the nightlife with mythical characters. Durrell demonised the city and depicted it as a prostitute. He got to know the wealthy, the educated foreign community members from whom he learned about local and Middle Eastern politics. His main fascinations were the girls in the brothels and the "*beau et nouveau-riche monde*" – their stories were what made his book seductive and intriguing. His famous quotation that Alexandria was "the great wine press of love" is known by many.

For those who visit Alexandria and want to find where Durrell lived for the last two years, from 1940 to 1942, it is to be found in a two-storey octagonal tower in the garden of the villa of the Ambron family in Mamoun Street, Moharrem Bey district. The Villa Ambron has been left to decay, despite interest by some celebrities and foreigners to buy and restore it, and restoration would be easy, as property in Alexandria is still relatively affordable.

During the last few weeks of his stay, Durrell walked "the dust-tormented streets where flies and beggars own it today", carrying Forster's book under his arm. I wonder if he, too, was fascinated more by the glorious ancient city than by modern Alexandria, which was changing from a European city into "the city of sorrows".

CHAPTER THREE

Reflections on Ancient Alexandria
Replacing the Famed Monuments on their Rightful Sites

During my student days, I would often sit at one of the cafeterias facing the coastal promenade and, on a perfect spring afternoon, it was appealing to be on the outskirts of the Grand Trianon to have a cup of tea and contemplate the total absence of archaeological remains from the Greek Ptolemaic civilisation. The electric tram terminal was on my right, and the setting sun was reflecting its rays onto the ochre walls of the buildings behind me, creating a soothing atmosphere. Above the Grand Trianon, three decades before, were the offices of the British Irrigation Company where Cavafy, the internationally-renowned poet, had worked for thirty years as a clerk in the early 1900s. Right in front of me would have been ancient Alexandria, the greatest achievement of the Greeks in Egypt, created by the first ruler, Ptolemy Lagos, childhood friend of Alexander. Both were tutored by Aristotle and, twelve years later, Lagos became Alexander's general, and Alexander's biographer in his old age.

Beginning my mental journey to place the ancient buildings, my starting point was the Silselah promontory on the east of the harbour – now reduced by land subsidence over the centuries to a narrow strip of land. In ancient times, this was a large peninsula named Cape Lochias, where the rulers built palaces and, at the southern end of Cape Lochias, was the "Gate of the Moon", a limestone archway forming the entrance to the city from the harbour.

The road leading from the "Gate of the Moon" to the south was Palace Street, intersecting with the Canopic Road, a large thoroughfare running from east to west. South of the peninsula was the palace district and the residential area of the Greeks known as the "Brucheion".

A landmark and tourist attraction close to the coastal promenade is the square of Saad Zaghloul, with a bronze statue of the nationalist leader who led a revolution in the early 1900s. It is on this exact site that Cleopatra built her palace in 42–41 BCE, called the Caesareiom in honour of the son she had with Julius Caesar. A good description of the palace is by Philo Judeus (a Jewish scholar and religious philosopher), written around 30–40 CE, who describes it as "a very large building, with series of paintings and statues all around leading to a vast precinct embellished with porticoes, gateways, groves, open terraces and courts". When Octavian, the Roman leader, entered Alexandria in 30 BCE, he was so impressed with this classic Greek building, with external decorations of two granite obelisks brought from Heliopolis, that he made it his home. These obelisks, called Cleopatra's needles, have survived because they were sent abroad as gifts from the Egyptian ruler during the 19th century: one to the United States in 1879 (now in Central Park, New York), and the other to Britain in 1877 (now on the London Embankment, opposite the Houses of Parliament).

Surprisingly, there are no remains of Cleopatra's magnificent palace. South of the Caesareiom was the Agora – the popular meeting place for Alexandrians – an elegantly decorated, colonnaded building with shops and enclosed areas for theatrical and gymnastic events. In Athens and Rome, the Agorae have been turned into open museums for locals and tourists but, in Alexandria, there is nothing left to be

Photograph of part of the city centre by the coast and Saad Zagoul Square.

seen. On the west of Saad Zaghloul Square and the Agora was the Emporium, which was active from the 2nd century BCE until the end of the Roman occupation. It housed the largest trading centre in the ancient world, dealing with grain, linen, glass, papyrus, pottery and cosmetics. Nowadays, shops, high-rise apartments, restaurants, cafeterias and patisseries cover the site of the old Emporium.

South of the Agora was the Soma (the Alexandrian term for the tomb of Alexander), which many archaeologists thought was situated at the intersection of Soma Street and Canopic Road. It is here that the Mosque of Nabi Daniel was built in the 15th century CE, and renovated during the 19th century. Despite many excavations being carried out during the renovation, and further separate searches recently, no evidence of Alexander's tomb or his sarcophagos have been found.

South of the Emporium was the Grand Library and Museum – the most significant part of the ancient city – where the seeds of modern science were sown and that history knows as "The School of Alexandria". When the Arabs occupied Alexandria in 645 CE, they were so impressed with its architecture, palaces and temples, that there is a phrase in the Koran describing the city as that "which has no like in the world".

Northwest of the eastern harbour was the island of Pharos, described in book 4 of Homer's 8th century BCE epic, *The Odyssey*. Alexander visited the area after he had dreamt that Homer spoke to him, which appears to be one of the reasons why he chose to build his capital city there, and suggested that a causeway should be constructed to link it to the coast.

Ptolemy I brought in Sostratos, an architect and builder from Caria in Ionia (southwest Asia Minor), to build a lighthouse on the eastern tip of Pharos Island (described in detail in chapter six of this volume). It survived attacks and natural disasters for 1,500 years and, when it eventually collapsed,

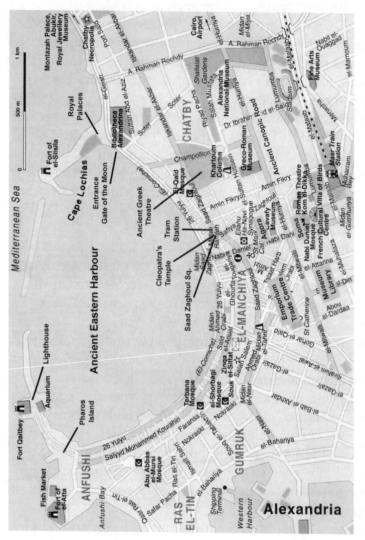

Map of modern Alexandria showing the ancient monuments on their original sites.

the Mameluke Sultan Kait Bey built a fort there to protect the city from the Ottoman Turks in 1480. Here, at least, there are visible signs of several huge stones from the original building. Close to the Fort of Kait Bey is the Greek Yacht Club, where we spent enjoyable weekends with family and friends during the summer months.

The Pharos peninsula, known in Arabic as *Ras al Tin* (Cape of Figs), has a naval museum and a palace built by the first viceroy in 1815. The causeway connecting Pharos Island to the mainland, called "Heptastadion" by the Greeks, now forms the densely-populated district of Mancheya.

My thoughts turned to the large thoroughfare, the ancient Canopic Road, which starts on the east at the "Gate of the Sun", in the modern suburb of Chatby, and ends at the western commercial harbour, Minet al Bassal, where, from 1840 until 1952, cotton was collected, stored and sorted by specialists according to quality, packed into bales and exported to England. The Canopic Road, twenty-seven-yards (twenty-five-metres) wide, was lined with columns and statues. Throughout the ages, its name has changed from Canopic to Rosetta, and now to El Horreya, the Arabic word for "liberation".

On the southwest of Lake Mareotis was the district of Rhakotis, where the Egyptians lived, and it was here that the Serapeion stood – known in antiquity as the largest and best-known temple of the deity for both Egyptian and Greeks. The idea was conceived by Ptolemy I, assisted by an Egyptian high priest named Manetho. Although Ptolemy I started the construction, it was completed and extended by Ptolemy III (Euergetes), who placed gold, silver and bronze foundation plaques at the corners, with inscriptions in both Greek and hieroglyphics. From archaeological investigation, it was found to be a rectangular building 190 yards (175 metres) long and eighty-eight yards (eighty metres) wide, with a row of columns supporting the roof, and rooms for accommodation in the eastern and southern parts of the temple. A few centuries later, the temple acted as a "daughter library" – a fact that was confirmed when later excavations found papyrus scrolls by Discorides, the 1st century Greek physician who wrote about medical substances.

In 391 CE, a Christian leader, Theophilos of Alexandria, declared war on "pagans" and destroyed the Serapeion.

The construction of houses and roads in ancient Alexandria was based on a grid system. With thoroughfares criss-crossing each other, this Greek model has been used in modern cities such as New York and Tokyo. It has been estimated that, during Ptolemy's I reign, seven thousand homes existed in Alexandria to house one hundred thousand people.

The Ptolemies had two harbours: the "Royal" on the east (used now for leisure boats) and the "Harbour of Good Return" on the west, used for commercial purposes, cotton and grain export.

On the hill north of the tram terminus, there was an ancient Greek theatre, popular with the Ptolemies, where tragic and comic plays were performed. It was on this site that the modern Alexandrians built their medical school and teaching hospital.

The Ptolemaic buildings in Alexandria had the Greek classic style, and some of the larger ones were two-storeyed with vaulted roof, arches and decorations. The ground floor of the buildings were Doric, the upper floor Ionic and the interior Corinthian, with some modifications.

Ptolemy is said to have built a wall around the city. There are some remains of the ancient wall by the Shallalat Gardens, and the Arab invaders used this as a starting point to build their own wall, shrinking the city. The confirmation that there was a Ptolemaic wall protecting the city comes from writings by Strabo, the geographer and historian, in his book *Geographia*, and from Kallimachos the poet, who mentions that the citizens used to ask whether they should congregate "inside" or "outside" the wall.

The ancient burial practice was to have the cemeteries outside the city walls. The Mustapha Pasha built, in the 3rd century BCE, highly-decorated tombs that are an example of this. The royal Ptolemaic tombs must have been inside the city walls for protection, and it is recorded by several historians that the last tomb of Alexander was built by Ptolemy IV (Philopator), close to the palace district.

Reflecting that nothing has survived of the Ptolemaic civilisation, except the name of the city, Alexander's image became a recurring thought.

In order to understand Alexander the Great – a global celebrity who, even after 2,300 years, is still a subject of discussion – it is essential to know about his education, achievements, iconography, cause of his death and legacy, without the elements of myth or fiction.

CHAPTER FOUR

Alexander III
The Great

*The Greek Macedonian king who conquered Persia in three battles
and spread Hellenic culture to the ancient world.*

Alexander was born in Pella, a populous, beautiful city and
capital of Macedonia, in the summer of 356 BCE. His father,
Philip II, claimed to be a descendant of Herakles (Hercules)
and to have inherited both his physical strength and character – a claim considerably increased by his unification of
the country's states and tribes within a short time.

Macedonia lies between the southern Balkans, with
Greece to the south and Asia to the east. The area is very
fertile, consisting of highlands and lowlands with rivers
irrigating the land, and an abundance of crops and cattle.
The Macedonians were Greek in language, culture and
thought.

Philip II was a most successful king, a highly efficient
military leader who organised an army more powerful than
that of any other Greek state. Under his leadership, the
Macedonian economy grew and the country became even
more prosperous than Athens and southern Greece. Philip's
busts portray him as thick-set, with a square jaw, a scar over
his right (blinded) eye, a beaked nose and a short, curly
beard. The ivory bust of Philip found in the royal tombs at
Vergina is probably by the sculptor Lysippos.

Alexander's mother, Olympias, was the daughter of King
Neoptolemos of the Molossians (a tribe from Epirus

province in northwest Greece) and claimed to be a descendant of Achilles. She was orphaned at an early age, and brought up by her uncle. An extant small medallion, found in Aboukir (west of Alexandria), shows her to be a handsome young woman who wore her hair in a Greek hairstyle, pulled back with a veil covering the back of her head. She was intelligent with a strong personality, had lofty morals, was politically ambitious, possessive, manipulative – and a mystic. Philip met Olympias at the celebration of the Cabeiri Mysteries at the Hieron of Samothraki (an island in the northern Aegean). He must have fallen in love but, to possess her, he had to marry her as premarital sex was unacceptable in Royal Macedonia and Greece.

Olympias had a bad marriage with Philip, who was both adulterous and polygamous, having married seven times. She was hurt, and knew that she had lost her position as the queen and mother of Alexander, the future king.

The Macedonians were united; the royal court was progressive with its own sculptors, painters and craftsmen who produced exquisite jewellery. Gold was available in the mountainous mass of Pangaion, northeast of Thessaloniki. Both father and son knew that they must unite the Greek states with Macedonia into one mighty army in order to invade their persistent enemy, Persia. Alexander was proud to be a descendant of Herakles via his father – a descendant of Achilles – and from his mother's ancestors, inheriting strength, bravery and invincibility. He was a prodigal child, intelligent, observant, remarkably brave, popular with everyone and made friends easily. Some remained life-long companions: Ptolemy, Hephaestion, Perdiccas and Krateros.

An example of young Alexander's powers of observation and bravery is the story about a wild, black Thessalian stallion named Bucephalas (ox-head), which was brought to the king by Philonikos of Thessaly for sale at a very high price. None of Philip's entourage –all experienced horsemen – could master the creature. Alexander observed that the stallion seemed to be afraid of his own shadow and those of the people around him, and asked his father's permission to try to tame the horse. He turned the stallion to face the sun, preventing him from seeing his shadow and those of the crowd and, when the horse stopped being restless, jumped onto its back and rode him with ease.

The king was overjoyed, and gave Alexander the stallion as a gift. For twenty years, Alexander used Bucephalas in most of his campaigns and even named a city after him in northeast Punjab.

Alexander's education

When Alexander was seven years old, his parents discussed his education and decided to bring Olympias' uncle, Leonidas of Epirus, to act as tutor and physical instructor. Leonidas forced Alexander to wear thin clothing, even during the cold winter months, and allowed him only two meals a day. He was very strict, even searching under Alexander's bedclothes to make sure that the family had not slipped him some treats. Alexander later blamed this strict regime for his short stature, as both his father and his childhood friend, Hephaestion, were taller. He was right: medical research has shown that, during childhood and adolescence, large amounts of dairy products containing calcium and protein are required for the development of the musculoskeletal system in order for children to grow tall.

Alexander was fortunate to have a manservant at his father's palace, Lysimachos, who attended him and told him stories about Achilles – even calling himself Phoenix who, in Homer's *Iliad*, was Achilles' tutor. Alexander began to think of himself as another Achilles. He remained grateful to Lysimachos for his devotion and never missed an opportunity to send him a gift from his campaigns. In fact,

Alexander's education and character made him a more sensitive person and a better soldier than Achilles.

Better years were ahead for Alexander when, at the age of thirteen, his father hired the wisest man in Greece – Aristotle, philosopher and scientist – to be his tutor. Philip chose a beautiful and peaceful site at Mieza (near modern Naoussa), in the foothills of the Vermion mountains north of Pella, where there was a country house called *Nymphaeum* ("shrine of the nymphs") to become a boarding school to educate Alexander and the sons of Macedonian noblemen.

Mieza was a sightseeing area known for its grottos. Surrounding the school were tall Macedonian pine and poplar trees, with a stream in the centre of a flower garden. Philip knew Aristotle personally, as he was the son of Nikomachos, physician to his father Amyntas III. When Aristotle arrived in Mieza, he was accompanied by his nephew Kallisthenes, a scholar who taught literature and history, and was later joined by another clever scholar, Theophrastus of Lesbos, who was the first botanist.

On arrival, Aristotle gave Alexander a gift – an old wooden box containing scrolls of Homer's epic poem, the *Iliad*, which had been transcribed and annotated by himself. Alexander must have been thrilled with this special gift, as these were the stories of the deeds of the ancient heroes, who suffered or paid a high price for their mistakes, that he knew from his childhood. When Alexander went on his campaigns to the East, he took with him this special copy of the *Iliad* and, it is said, slept with the scroll under his pillow. Later, he kept it safe in a golden box acquired after defeating Darius III, emperor of Persia, at the Battle of Issos.

Alexander considered Homer to be the perfect storyteller – both a historian and a military strategist. Aristotle and Kallisthenes introduced their pupils to Hesiod, Pindar and Xenophon. Alexander enjoyed Xenophon's *Cyropaedia*, which tells the story of Cyrus II, founder of Persia, considered to be the role model of a wise ruler. They studied the Greek tragedies of Aeschylos, Euripides, Sophocles and the comic poet Aristophanes. Aeschylos was an optimistic moralist – his *Oresteia* trilogy was considered by the Athenians to be a noble play, the rejoicing of triumph and hope over despair.

Aristotle's favourite play was Sophocles' *Antigone,* and Alexander also knew Euripides' plays well. Aristophanes' plays carried a political and religious message, and were entertaining with a mixture of comedy and burlesque.

Aristotle taught philosophy, combining the theory and application of practical knowledge, logic, ethics, law, politics, literature, botany and medicine. From a young age, Alexander was interested in science to the extent that, whilst away on his campaigns in Asia, he sent specimens of plants to the Lyceum (Aristotle's school in Athens) for study, and used some of his knowledge of medicine to look after his wounded soldiers.

He learned from Aristotle that the basic requirements for a good life were to be free, to have just laws and to enjoy the Hellenic lifestyle: music, theatre and celebratory victories with athletic games after battle. The major differences in opinion between pupil and teacher were that Aristotle believed captured men should be treated as slaves, while captured women should be accepted as second-class citizens. Alexander had great difficulty in accepting these views. There are examples of this: Alexander respected the peoples and cultures of the countries that he conquered, and wished to negate any attitudes of western supremacy. He was particularly protective to women, who were vulnerable to his conquering soldiers, and he proved to be more caring than his teacher.

It was in Mieza that Alexander developed a close relationship with Hephaestion, son of Amyntoros, who became his constant companion and supreme commander of his forces. Aristotle and his assistants taught in Mieza for approximately four years, until Alexander was seventeen years old. For his tuition fee, he asked Philip II to rebuild his birthplace, Stagira (a city on the coast of Thrace, east of Macedonia); the king agreed and the city was beautifully restored. Alexander had the very best education, with teachers of science, philosophy and literature, and the finest physical education from the experienced generals of his father's army.

After Alexander had finished his studies, his father left to fight yet another war and declared his son regent of Macedonia, at the age of seventeen. The more lands that Philip conquered, the better the economic growth and the greater the security of the country. Alexander's first military assignment was to quell a rebellion in a region near present Bulgaria. He was victorious, renaming the town Alexandropolis – imitating his father's habit of naming the cities that he conquered. He fought alongside his father in Thrace, where his outstanding bravery was so evident that his father promoted him to general. This was a good time for both father and son, fighting in battle together and getting to know each other.

Unexpectedly, Philip fell in love with the daughter of a Macedonian nobleman and married her. This event created great concern about Alexander's accession to the throne, as his mother, Olympias, was not a Macedonian, and a male child from this new marriage would affect Alexander's succession.

Despite his father's recent marriage, the bond between father and son remained strong and, in 338 BCE, Philip and Alexander fought together against the Greeks at the Battle of Chaeronea, in Boeotia. Their victory contributed to defeating the confederation of Greek city states, and Macedonia became the undisputed military power. The League of Corinth was formed by the Greek city states, without Sparta, and they unanimously appointed King Philip II of Macedonia to assume leadership of the pan-

Hellenic league's forces. It took more than two years of military preparations for the united armies to prepare for their campaign against Persia.

The murder of his father, Philip II

A tragic event occurred during this period when, at the wedding of Cleopatra (daughter of Philip and Olympias), the king was stabbed to death by his bodyguard, Pausanias, as he entered the theatre to attend the celebratory wedding games. Pausanias was chased and killed by the guards whilst escaping, and two other accomplices were found guilty and executed. The death of Philip II devastated Alexander, and the whole of Greece.

After his father's death, Alexander was proclaimed king at the age of twenty, in 336 BCE. He organised his father's funeral pyre, supervised the rites and appointed architects, builders and artists to construct and decorate Philip's tomb. After he had completed these necessary social duties, he travelled to Corinth, where he was well received by the League and was given his deceased father's position – the leadership of the pan-Hellenic league's forces.

Alexander had inherited from his father a formidable, well-trained and loyal army. With the united forces, he marched through northern Greece and crossed the Hellespont into Asia Minor, stopping to lay a wreath on the graves of Achilles and Patroclos in northwest modern Turkey. In the spring of 334 BCE, he won his first victory over the Persians at the Battle of the Granicus River. In November of that year, at the Battle of Issos, he again defeated the Persians, liberating Greek Asia Minor. This was the most significant victory for Alexander who, at the age of twenty-four, had succeeded in liberating Asia Minor and overwhelming Emperor Darius III of Persia, who fled leaving his family behind. Alexander showed respect for the abandoned royal family, and took Darius' mother, Sisygambis, and his wife and children under his personal protection.

There is a descriptive work by the Venetian artist Veronese, painted in 1567, showing the Darius family kneeling in front of Hephaestion, mistaking him for Alexander. Legend has it that, when Alexander realised Sisygambis' embarrassment, he bent over and whispered to her: "Do not be concerned mother – he, too, is an Alexander." This painting hangs in Room 9 of the National Gallery in London, and has been one of the many stimuli for me while writing the biography of Alexander.

After his victory at Issos, Alexander marched into Syria and Phoenicia (present-day Lebanon) where the Persians had their naval base. He met a lot of resistance in Tyre but, with help from other cities under his control, the Tyrians could resist no longer and Alexander was victorious once again – keeping his reputation that he never lost a battle. He moved on to Gaza and Philistine (the ancient land west of the River Jordan, renamed by the British to Palestine). From there, he entered Egypt through Sinai, reaching the holy pharaonic city of Memphis in 332 BCE.

The first thing he did was to show his respect to the god Ptah by carrying out a ritual of sacrifice – something that no other conqueror of Egypt had done before. The Egyptian high priests and nobility must have been impressed with Alexander, who showed understanding and sensitivity to the beliefs of others, and hailed him as their liberator from the oppressive Persians, proclaiming him pharaoh of Upper and Lower Egypt. This incident is verified on an ancient Egyptian sanctuary wall at Luxor that depicts Alexander as a pharaoh facing the god Min.

Alexander founding his city in Egypt, and his trip to the Oracle of Amun

Alexander sailed northwards from Memphis, through the western tributary of the Nile delta, and stopped opposite the island of Pharos – following the instructions he remembered from his dream while in Egypt. On reaching the island, he must have been disappointed to find it was too small for settlement, and that the land between the wide sea and Lake Mareotis was a hilly strip of desert land stretching from east to west.

Despite his poor initial impression, he declared that the area was his choice to build a city to bear his name. He drew a plan of the city in the shape of a stretched Macedonian *chlamys* (mantle), two miles (3.2 kilometres) in diameter, and suggested that the island should be connected to the mainland by building a causeway, thus converting it into a peninsula and dividing the large harbour into two. For a young man, Alexander must have had some knowledge of town planning, learned from either Aristotle or Hippodamus, who had designed the port of Piraeus.

Why did Alexander select this particular plot of land, to the west of the Nile, to build his city? The already-established towns and ports of Canopos and Herakleion, which had flourished as trading centres in the 5th century BCE, connecting the Aegean with Egypt through the Nile tributaries, lay by the Bay of Aboukir, seventeen miles (twenty-five kilometres) further east. There must have been many reasons for his selection of this site. First and foremost, Alexander had seen a grey-haired man in his dream, who quoted from Homer's *Odyssey* (book 4): "There is an island in the middle of the abounding sea in front of Egypt, Pharos they call it . . . with a safe harbour sheltering it from the winds." Alexander was convinced that the old man was Homer. A second, and important, reason was his unexpected welcome by the Egyptian hierarchy who hailed him as their liberator from the Persians.

There were, of course, practical reasons too: geographically, it was an ideal location – a large natural harbour, Greece to the north, Asia to the east and Europe to the west, with a good climate, abundant fresh water from the Nile river, and plenty of grain and cattle – making it an ideal area to start a city and port. He appointed a local Greek, Kleomenes, as governor, and Deinokrates as architect and town planner, specifying that the city be built in a classic Greek architectural design that also blended harmoniously with the pharaonic Egyptian style.

Alexander stayed in Egypt for two to three months. Before leaving for Persia, he wished to consult personally with the priests of the Oracle of Amun (Zeus), located at the Oasis of Siwa in the western desert, near the border with Libya. His reason for the trip was to ask two questions: first, how successful would he be in his future military campaigns and, second, about his possible divinity, as his mother had told him from childhood that he was divine. The Oracle of Amun was known to the Greeks because the first two pilgrims to visit it were Perseus and Herakles – no Egyptian pharaoh had ever visited the site.

The journey from Alexandria to Siwa was a long and hazardous four hundred miles (650 kilometres). Alexander, with his close companions Hephaestion, Ptolemy, Krateros, Kallisthenes (his official historian) and Eumenes (his secretary), accompanied by soldiers, travelled along the Mediterranean coast to the west where, twenty-three centuries later, Alexandrians would spend their summer holidays on the remote beaches of Agami, El Alamein and Marsa Matruh (the modern name for Paraetonion). From Paraetonion, they journeyed south through the desert to Siwa, encountering many problems, including a severe sandstorm, running short of water and then losing their way. After a few days, the sandstorm cleared. It then poured with rain, and a flock of crows –the "birds of Apollo" – flew in front of them, leading them safely to the oasis. On reaching the oracle, the high priest welcomed Alexander and bid him to enter alone. There are two recorded versions of what happened: the first is that, as the high priest spoke some Greek, he may have called Alexander *paidion* ("my child"); the second is that he said *pai-dios* ("son of Zeus"), which Alexander may have taken as meaning that he *was* divine. Inside the oracle, the high priest responded to the questions asked. When Alexander came out, his friends expected to hear sensational news but he simply said that the answers to his questions "were what he wished to hear".

Kallisthenes, his secretary, had already declared Alexander's divinity well before the trip, and it is unfortunate that it was he who later fell foul of Alexander when he criticised him for adopting *proskynesis* (Persian customs of respect), such as bowing in front of the king and kissing his hand. When Kallisthenes refused to conform, he was accused of treason and executed. We do not know whether Alexander was convinced of his divinity but, when he became the great king of Asia after conquering Persia, his subjects (except the Greeks and Macedonians) treated him as divine.

Alexander took a different route for the return journey, travelling eastwards through the desert and resting halfway at the Bahariya Oasis, which was uninhabited at that time. In 1938, excavations at Bahariya revealed a temple and burial place dedicated to Alexander and, in 1996, more burials were found in a very large cemetery, now known as the "Golden Mummies". The cemetery must have been built by the Ptolemies and, over the centuries, had become a cult visited by Egyptians, Greeks, Romans and Christians, who even buried their own dead there. Alexander rested in Bahariya and reflected on his successful trip to the Oracle of Amun, exhilarated and looking forward to conquering Persia.

Alexander's iconography and Hellenic artists

King Philip II asked Lysippos of Sikyon, a Greek sculptor, to make busts of his son Alexander whilst he was being taught by Aristotle in Mieza. Lysippos spent time studying the boy and got to know him well, making a lot of bronze sculptures, but none of them have been found. The most celebrated bust – the Azara herm of Alexander – is a Roman copy in marble from an original bronze by Lysippos. It was found by the Spanish ambassador to Italy, Jose Nicola d'Azara, in Rome's Tivoli Gardens in 1779, and was given as a gift to the Emperor Napoleon. It is now on display in the Paris Louvre. The base of the marble bust has an inscription, "Alexander, son of Philip", and the features are symmetrical, with the hair standing up in the centre, large eyes and slightly open mouth.

In the British Museum in London, there is another marble bust that was found in Alexandria, having similar features to the Azara herm. The ivory figurine heads of Philip, Olympias, Alexander and a fourth person, found in Philip's tomb in Vergina, are most probably by Lysippos. His other recorded sculptures in bronze, known as "Apoxyomenos", are those of an athlete scraping oil from his body with a curved instrument called a *strigil*.

There are three features of Lysippos' work that made him an innovative and influential sculptor of the period, and were later copied during the Renaissance: first, the rotation of the torso, giving the impression of natural movement; second, the size of the head in proportion to the body, which he changed from the standard ratio of 1:7 to 1:8, so as not to increase the actual height of the statue but to make the figure appear tall and gracious; and, third, Lysippos made the arms and knees project forward. Michelangelo must have been influenced by Lysippos when he sculpted his marble statue of David in Florence.

In most of the busts, Alexander is portrayed as having

handsome, symmetrical features, clean-shaven, with some prominence of the forehead, a leonine mane of hair, large eyes with an upwards glance, a thin, hooked nose and tilting of the neck with rotation of the head. As a young man, we cannot be sure that Alexander had in mind a specific image of himself, but it has been reported that he liked the way Lysippos portrayed him, showing his good looks, strength, with the poise of the neck turning to the left and an aspiring glance.

During Philip and Alexander's reigns, there were several notable painters: Aetion, Apelles, Protogenes, Nikomachos, Philoxenos and Antiphilos. Aetion painted the *Marriage of Alexander and Roxane*, which Raphael (the Renaissance Italian painter) used as the theme for his 1517 painting to adorn the walls of the Villa Farnesina in Rome. The original painting was described by Loukianos (Lucian) of Samosata, Syria (117–180 CE), who spent some time in Alexandria, in his book *Ekphrasis*.

Antiphilos, another Greek artist born in Egypt, painted Alexander in childhood in *The Hunt of Ptolemy* and in a painting of "a child blowing on a flame", which influenced the Cretan artist Domenicos Theotokopoulos (El Greco) when he painted the same subject in 1575. The picture now hangs in the Prado Museum in Madrid, Spain.

Apelles of Kolophon (in Asia Minor) was Alexander's official painter and friend but, unfortunately, none of his paintings have survived. It is said that his portrait of Alexander as Zeus was so perfect that the fingers holding the thunderbolt seemed to protrude and the lightning stood out from the picture! Alexander asked him to paint his girl-friend, Campaspe, nude. When he realised that she had captured the artist's heart, he offered her to him. For European artists, Apelles was considered the pioneer of "verism" (true painting). After some Renaissance artists read the stories about Campaspe, many adopted the theme of including Apelles with her in the presence of Alexander.

The most famous versions are by Tiepolo, Vleughles and J. A. Winghe, but my favourite is by Sebastiano Ricci, displayed in the National Gallery of Parma, Italy, which shows Alexander standing in military clothes, Apelles – with a very happy expression – leaning backwards on his chair whilst painting Campaspe sitting fully dressed with the facial features of Aphrodite.

There are many legends about Greek painters, and a special one is about Apelles' visit to Protogenes, a painter and sculptor famous for his two *Sacred Triremes* (Paralus and Hammonias) that were on display in the Propylaea of the Acropolis in Athens. Apelles went to see Protogenes at his home in Rhodes, but could not find him, so he drew a very thin, dark line across a plain panel as if he was leaving his visiting card. When Protogenes returned, he realised that this line must have been drawn by a friend, and himself drew another, thinner, line just above, it in a different colour and without leaving a space. The next day, Apelles returned again, but Protogenes was still not there. This time, he drew an even thinner line between them, in a lighter colour. From this story of the lines drawn by Apelles and Protogenes, it seems that they made a major contribution to western art, the perspective of objects in space, mass through light and shadow, and the use of lustre and highlights that bring a shape forwards.

Apelles also painted Aphrodite rising from the sea, squeezing the water from her wet hair with sparkling highlights. Botticelli, the Italian Renaissance painter, must have read about this and painted Venus floating on a seashell.

In 1977, Manolis Andronikos, the Greek archaeologist, discovered three tombs in Vergina (ancient Aegae), in the foothills of the Pieria Mountains, southwest of Thessaloniki. When he presented his findings to the Royal Academy in London, he became a celebrity in the western world. The smallest tomb was found empty because it had been plundered, suggesting that the contents must have been precious. A well-preserved painting was found on the walls, depicting the abduction of Persephone by Hades (Pluto), the god of the Underworld.

On the north wall, the dramatic main scene shows Hades standing in his chariot, his right hand holding the reins and his left hand grasping Persephone tightly above the waist. It shows her panic-stricken face with wide-open eyes, her body taught, both arms and legs extended, as if in spasm, and her purple gown covering only the lower part of her body. Hades' face is remarkable, looking determined with large, piercing eyes (a characteristic of paintings of the period). On the eastern wall, Persephone's mother, Demetra (the "earth mother"), representing the fertile soil, is depicted looking desperate and sitting on a stone. On the south wall, a well-preserved scene shows the Three Fates – Clotho, the spinner of life; Lachesis, the element of luck or chance; and Atropos, the inescapable fate. This tomb has been named Persephone's Room, and is the longest wall painting found in ancient Greece. Experts have concluded that it was probably by Nikomachos of Thebes. In the 4th century BCE, a copy of this painting was displayed at the Temple of Athena in the Capitolium in Rome, as reported by Pliny (Natural History 35).

Southwest of Persephone's Room is a large, intact building consisting of two rooms. At the main entrance, there is a frieze above the door with another masterpiece: a painting of a hunting scene in a forest. Alexander features on horseback, easily identifiable on the frieze with a wreath on his head, large, prominent eyes and, in his right hand, a spear. This painting also shows an older man on horseback, with a square jaw and large nose, carrying a spear ready to kill a lion; it is assumed that this is Philip, and that father and son are shown hunting together.

In 1831, a mosaic, depicting Alexander facing Darius at the Battle of Issos, was found at the House of the Faun in Pompeii, and is on display at the National Museum in

Naples. Very likely, it was copied from an original painting by Philoxenos of Eritrea, commissioned for his tomb by King Kassander of Macedonia around 317 BCE. This painting, on the frieze of the entrance of the tomb, must be attributed to Philoxenos because of the similar facial features of Alexander compared to those on the mosaic of the Battle of Issos. The personal belongings and other items found in the chamber have been identified as belonging to Philip II.

Before the discovery of these Macedonian tombs with their wall paintings, the art world knew only of Greek paintings on vases. The wall paintings in Vergina showed that, during the great age of Alexander and the subsequent Hellenistic period after his death, new techniques had developed showing perspective, facial expression and movement. Later, the artists of the Renaissance showed, through their copies, the importance of this innovative work.

The task of designing engraved images on gems and coins was given to Pyrgoteles, and some of his work has survived. The quality of his work was so precise that the coins and gems propagated Alexander's influence for centuries after his death. In 300 BCE, silver and gold coins of Alexander circulated, portraying him as Zulqarnain, with the two horns of Amun around his ears to depict his divinity.

The death of Alexander and his legacy

Alexander spent several months in Babylon, working and planning for his new expeditions to the west. In his diary, his secretary, Eumenes, recorded that there were many drinking parties before Alexander's illness and death. Medios, a personal companion, had invited him to a party where at least twenty friends had gathered. It was also reported that the person who offered the toast to honour Alexander, and gave him a drinking cup, was Proteus, whose uncle, Kleitos, Alexander had killed in anger a few months before. When Alexander swallowed the drink, he screamed with acute pain, immediately feeling unwell and leaving the party to return to his quarters. His condition gradually deteriorated, despite having treatment from his physician and constant nursing care by his wife Roxane, and he died ten days later. Before his death, during one of his lucid periods, Alexander gave Perdiccas (his trusted commander-in-chief) his signet ring, and placed Roxane's hand in his, indicating that he should protect her.

It is surprising that none of the people around him – Ptolemy, who kept a diary, Aristovoulos, his architect and trusted friend, or his personal secretary, Eumenes –described any specific symptoms or signs. If we knew a little more of the progress of his symptoms: fever, constant pain, vomiting, diarrhoea, and skin eruptions, a diagnosis of salmonella infection could be considered – which, if untreated, may lead to perforation of the bowel and death. Other diagnoses, such as an acute gastric ulcer or perforated appendix, can lead to peritonitis, septicaemia and death.

Alexander's biographers and historians have suggested that he died of acute alcoholism, but the clinical presentation is totally different, starting with muscular incoordination and leading to mental disturbance and, eventually, death. The common symptoms of malaria associated with *plasmodium vivax* and *plasmodium ovale* is fever, with rigors when the temperature rises, hot flushes (recurring every day), and death occurring mostly in children, not adults. However, the malarial symptoms associated with *plasmodium falciparum* are more complex, starting with malaise, headache, vomiting and confusion, and ending with kidney failure, shock and death. In Alexander's case, malaria can be excluded.

Poisoning must be seriously considered, as many people wanted Alexander dead. First and foremost was Proteus, whose uncle had been killed by Alexander. Another suspect was Antipater, regent of Macedonia, who disliked Alexander and sent his son, Kassander, to Babylon, for an unknown reason, a few weeks before Alexander's illness. Another coincidence is that Antipater's other son, Iollas, was present as Alexander's cupbearer.

The most common poison available in ancient Greece was hellebore, used as a drug in very small doses. There are two varieties – black and white – both of which, when given over a number of days, produce acute pain, vomiting, delirium, muscle spasm and death. It is possible that those who came to visit Alexander in Babylon, a few days before his death, could have brought hellebore or strychnine and put it into Alexander's drink. When Alexander's mummified body is eventually found, endoscopic examination of the stomach (gastroscopy) will reveal the cause of death.

In the Palace of Nebuchadnezzar in Babylon, there is a clay tablet bearing the date of Alexander's death in June 323 BCE. On hearing the news of his death, his troops and the people of Babylon became numb and unable to do anything, "even light a candle". Throughout Persia, the country he had conquered, citizens went into mourning – some even shaved their heads – and the mother of Darius, Sisygambis, starved herself while, in Greece, his allies started an uprising against the Macedonians.

After Alexander's death, the prospect of the survival of a Greek empire in the East was gradually vanishing. The post-Alexander period was called Hellenistic, with new kingdoms in the East at Antioch, Seleucia, Pergamon, Syria and – greatest of all – the city of Alexandria on the Mediterranean coast of Egypt.

During the period of mourning in various Asiatic and Persian territories, preparations began in Babylon to construct Alexander's funeral carriage. His body was embalmed like all the pharaohs and placed in a hammered-gold anthropoid sarcophagus shaped to fit his body. The funeral carriage took two years to complete and needed a large number of mules to pull it. The vaulted roof of the carriage was supported by Ionic columns and decorated with scales of mother-of-pearl and semi-precious stones; below the edge of the ceiling was a cornice with four painted panels, depicting Alexander and three battle scenes from his campaigns. The spaces between the columns were filled with golden netting to screen the body and, all around the carriage, there were bells that could be heard when travelling so people could come and pay their respects. It must have been the most spectacular funeral carriage ever made.

The funeral procession was to travel from Babylon to Aegae (modern Vergina), where the kings of Macedonia were traditionally buried. However, Ptolemy, son of Lagos, thought that Alexander's body should be buried in Egypt, so the first thing he did was to get rid of Kleomenes and appoint himself as ruler of Egypt. For the city to have royal status and prestige, he needed Alexander's body to reinforce his position and please the Egyptians – by bringing back their pharaoh they, in turn, would support him in building a city worthy of Alexander.

Ptolemy travelled with an army to Syria to meet the funeral carriage, which was heading north. After a battle with Perdiccas's soldiers, he hijacked the carriage, took possession of the body and headed to Memphis in Egypt. On hearing the news that the funeral carriage had been hijacked, Perdiccas, the commander-in-chief, joined his troops to face Ptolemy in Egypt and reclaim the body but, during the trip, he was killed by one of his generals.

Alexander's body is said to have been placed in Memphis, in an empty green-stone sarcophagus with hieroglyphics that had been intended for Nectanebo II, the last pharaoh. There it remained for safekeeping for four or five decades. The first tomb was built by Ptolemy II, but the second (and final) one, a magnificent tomb in the palace area, was constructed by Ptolemy IV.

To both ancient and modern Greeks, the English-speaking world and to educated Asians and Arabs, Alexander was the prototype of a conqueror who brought civilisation and spread Greek culture to the East. By the age of eighteen, he was an accomplished soldier and, until the end of his life, he had never lost a battle in ten years of fighting. He became the model of a military man and a heroic king, liberating Asia Minor and conquering Persia in the three battles of Granicus, Issos and Gaugamela. There is ample evidence that he respected the religions and customs of the countries he invaded. When in Egypt, he visited Memphis and paid his respects to the Egyptian gods; when he conquered Persia, he did the same and even adopted some of their customs. He was considerate to women and respectful to defeated kings, and proved this when he took care of the Persian royal family – the mother, wife and children of King Darius who had left his family behind when he was defeated in battle.

Alexander read literature, including the Homeric epics and Athenian plays, as well as practical subjects such as town planning, irrigation and agriculture – books that were available as the Greeks had the excellent habit of recording their knowledge. He encouraged people to work hard, cultivate the soil, respect their parents and care for them. He rebuilt many cities with the knowledge and experience that he had acquired, with the aim that conquered countries should recover and prosper.

Alexander reformed the economy of the conquered states by starting the movement of monies using silver instead of gold, as the value of gold could fluctuate. He used the Persian idea of decimalisation and converted one gold Persian unit into twenty silver pieces. In the years after his death, the economies improved by more than several hundred percent in Greece, Macedonia and Persia. The economic realities were good, and the money was used to maintain the army and an expanding navy. However, after many years with a large amount of silver money circulating, inflation occurred in countries that traded large amounts of grain and other commodities. The cities that he created in Persia had humane laws and were well run, the inhabitants learnt the Greek language, classics and art, and everything was made by craftsmen, even down to the smallest item of jewellery or coin.

Alexander's personal life is not easy to analyse, as he spent ten years fighting without rest, which must have had an effect on his behaviour and personality. In the Greek city states and Macedonia, homosexuality in young men was not as common as the western world likes to present. The natural sexual freedom of the ancient Greeks was a result of their enlightened ideas, without any religious prohibition. On vase drawings, young men are shown fondling each other, but anal sex was scorned. Homosexuality did exist among a small number of older, single men, but there was a stigma attached to those who practised it. Male prostitution was against the Athenian law and, if caught, they could lose their citizenship. Recent biographers and filmmakers have made an issue of homosexuality in ancient Greece, especially with Alexander, for the sake of creating sensationalism. His secretary, Eumenes, recorded that Alexander was displeased when people offered him young men at parties "to have fun with", and there is no recorded evidence that he enjoyed homosexual liaisons. Alexander, as a young man, had a child with Barsine, a Persian woman, and he had a harmonious marriage with Roxane, who bore him a son. After conquering Persia, he married the daughter of Darius for political reasons.

There is historical evidence that Alexander's character started to change in the year that Persepolis was destroyed (330 BCE), and he became suspicious that his own friends were betraying him – Philotas was executed for treason, while his closest friend, Kleitos, was killed by Alexander during an argument. The continuous fighting for ten years had brought him both absolute power and exhaustion, and his attitudes hardened.

Ancient Greek religion suited the character of the Greeks, as they did not have to conform to a specific dogma and were allowed freedom of thought and tolerance – indeed, many considered the gods to be an ingenious allegory. However, Alexander himself was religious – it has been recorded that he regularly sacrificed to the gods before battles and when he was injured or felt unwell. His trip to the Oracle of Amun proved he was a genuine believer.

Historically, the Macedonian kings (including Alexander's grandfather, Amyntas) were worshipped in shrines, and it was said that the man who would conquer Persia deserved "the glory equal to that of a god". Eumenes recorded a few of Alexander's future plans: the conquest of Arabia, a road from Alexandria along the coast of North Africa to the Pillars of Herakles at Gibraltar and, after this, campaigns in western Europe. He had planned to build new and great cities with manpower and resources from Asia, and to allow transmigration of people from other countries – the beginning of globalisation.

Alexander's most important legacies must be the fulfilment of his father's ambition to unite Macedonia with the Greek city states, and his successful conquest of Persia. He founded many cities in order to have Hellenistic governments and institutions, opening trading routes to encourage prosperous lifestyles for their citizens. Alexandrian merchants were found everywhere, and Greek influence through language, literature and art lasted for six hundred years – well after the Romans had left. Hellenistic leaders invaded India and opened the silk route, while Greek art spread to the extent that some Buddhist sculptors changed Buddha's facial expression to resemble that of Alexander.

Christianity and Islam rose in Hellenistic lands, and both religions benefited from Greek philosophical influences. In 391 CE, the Christians attacked pagan temples; paradoxically, some of them wore Alexander amulets, thus believing in the invincibility and divinity of a pagan. The Prophet Mohammed pronounced Alexander as a prophet along with Moses and Jesus, as mentioned in the Koran (*Sura al Kahaf* 18). The image of Zulqarnain, "the two-horned lord", is identified as Alexander by the Arabs and has been reproduced on their coins, while Egyptian Christians used his name on their religious tapestries several centuries later.

Alexander was interested in exploring different countries and encouraged others to do the same. An example of this is Pytheas of Ionia. In 300 BCE, he travelled to France and founded Massalia (Marseille), from where he sailed to Britain and founded the tin mines in Cornwall, before going further north, to Scotland and the Isles, and as far as Iceland.

In summary, Alexander's legacy was the spread of Hellenic knowledge and art, the exchange of culture between East and West, and encouraging marriage between Macedonians, Greeks and Persians, hoping that it might bring peace. The city of Alexandria on the Mediterranean coast of Egypt was the most successful of all his cities, and the site of the world's first university, which carried out research into mathematics, science and medicine, as well as influencing religious thinking during the first three centuries of Christianity.

CHAPTER FIVE

The Quest for the Elusive Tomb of Alexander the Great

Since 300 CE, there has been consistent interest in the whereabouts of Alexander's tomb and sarcophagos. The Alexandrians hoped that he was buried "under our feet" somewhere in the city centre – a subject that became a topic of conversation for the locals from the late 1930s until 1956, while sitting at the Elite café-restaurant where the waiter, Stelios Koumoutsos, was obsessed with finding Alexander's burial place.

In order to make our search for the tomb orderly and scientific, the facts must be put into chronological order. After Alexander's death in Babylon, his body was embalmed as a pharaoh, although Macedonian kings were usually cremated. His golden sarcophagos was shaped to his body and a spectacular funeral carriage was built to carry it. The procession was scheduled to travel from Babylon to Syria, and on to Aegae – the burial place of Macedonian royalty. The new ruler of Egypt, Ptolemy, son of Lagos, hijacked the sarcophagus and took it through the desert to Memphis, the ancient capital of Egypt south of the Nile delta, for both safekeeping and for political prestige.

West of Memphis is the Temple of Osiris and Apis at Sakkara, and it was there that Alexander's body was placed. The event of bringing the body to be buried in Memphis is chronicled on the Parian Marble under the date of 321–320 BCE. The Parian Marble is a unique and precious piece of inscribed marble that selectively covers historical events from 1581–264 BCE. In 1627, the largest fragment of the chronicle was found in Smyrna, Asia Minor, and is now at the Ashmolean Museum in Oxford, England. In 1897, a smaller piece, consisting of thirty-two lines, was found on a plot of land belonging to the Ellie Varouha family in Tholos, Parikia, and was donated to the local archaeological museum of Paros.

Whilst attending an orthopaedic meeting in Oxford, it was convenient for me to visit the Ashmolean Museum to study this larger fragment. On returning to Greece, I discussed with an Alexandrian schoolmate from Victoria College, who was then a consultant with the European Union (EU) in Brussels, whether, through the EU and the British, we could ask the Ashmolean to make us a copy of their Parian fragment. Correspondence started with the curator, who was very considerate and helpful and, three years later, a large parcel arrived in Paros, containing a copy of the larger fragment! It is now proudly displayed in the Archaeological Museum of Paros, next to our smaller fragment. This gesture from the curator of the Ashmolean Museum shows that cultural cooperation between England and Greece is possible and can be beneficial to both countries, giving us hope that other important artefacts can be exchanged between Britain and Greece.

After four decades, Ptolemy II (Philadelphus) brought Alexander's body to Alexandria to bury him in a tomb in the city centre – the site of which is still undiscovered. In 215 BCE, Ptolemy IV (Philopater), after winning the Battle of Raphia, near Gaza, decided to honour Alexander by building a large family tomb for the other three deceased rulers, along with a separate area in which to place Alexander's sarcophagos. It is reported that this second tomb was circular, similar to some sacred buildings in ancient Greece, which were always highly decorated with statues all around, but this tomb was subterranean. Again, the site of this tomb has not been found, although it is highly probable that it was close to the main gardens and palaces of the Ptolemies.

Around 93 BCE, Ptolemy X, needing money to pay his army, plundered Alexander's tomb, removing the body from the golden sarcophagus and placing him in a glass or alabaster coffin. This so enraged the citizens that he was exiled to Cyprus, where he died – probably murdered – sometime later.

The Roman poet Lucan (36–65 CE), in his epic unfinished poem *Pharsalia*, relates the account of the civil war between Caesar and Pompey, and describes the visit of Julius Caesar to the city and to Alexander's tomb in 48 BCE. Describing it as having a circular roof decorated with statues, in order to view Alexander the Great, Caesar had to go down steps – thus confirming that the tomb was subterranean.

A second visitor to the tomb was Caesar's successor, Octavian. In 30 BCE, after entering Alexandria, he visited the tomb and placed a golden wreath on Alexander's head –accidentally breaking the mummified nose. Another visitor, in 25 BCE, was Strabo the geographer, who described the tomb only as a "walled enclosure in the city centre". There are also recorded visits by Emperor Hadrian, in 130 CE, who may have been inspired by the tomb's cylindrical shape and copied the design for his own monument in Rome, the Castel Saint Angelo. Emperor Caracalla also visited the tomb, in 210 CE, but there is no mention of the sarcophagus. Much later, in 361 CE, Ammianus Marcellinus, a Greek traveller living in Rome, described the tomb as "splendid" but made no mention of its location.

From this evidence, it is clear that many people visited the tomb after Caesar's visit in 48 BCE, and continued up to 361 CE, but there has been no recorded sighting of the tomb since then. One possible explanation for this would be that, if the tomb was close to the coast, it may have been submerged during the earthquake of 365 CE.

When Napoleon III was visiting Alexandria in 1861, he asked Khedive Ismail, ruler of Egypt, to find a scholar with knowledge of the city to draw a map of ancient Alexandria. The person chosen was Mahmoud Bey al Falaki, an engineer and town planner educated in France, who accepted the project and produced a map that became the standard reference of the ancient city. It was unfortunate that al Falaki suggested that Alexander's tomb was under the Mosque of Nabi Daniel, at the intersection of two roads in the city centre, as this started many fruitless searches. The mosque had been partly built in the 15th century CE, and was completed during the rule of Mohammed Ali in the early 19th century. If the tomb of Alexander had been under the mosque, it would have been located during the construction. The mosque was built in reverence to both the Prophet Daniel and a local holy person, Sidi Lokman, and it was their tombs that were preserved under the building – al Falaki had wrongly assumed that one of the subterranean tombs he saw under the mosque was that of Alexander.

In 1908, the archaeologist and director of the Greco–Roman Museum in Alexandria, Evaristo Breccia, excavated a site close to the Italian cemetery in Chatby, where there were large blocks of alabaster, suggestive of a tomb. However, he was not convinced that it had anything to do with Alexander, and abandoned the project. However, Achille Adriani, the archaeologist who succeeded Breccia, was curious about the alabaster tomb and restarted excavation, whereupon he found more alabaster blocks and used them to reconstruct a two-room building similar to the royal tombs in Macedonia. It is possible that Ptolemy II (Philadelphus) had brought Alexander from Memphis in the empty green-stone sarcophagus of Nectanebo II, and buried him in this alabaster area until Ptolemy IV built the circular tomb by the palace district.

When the Arabs occupied Alexandria in 645 CE, they built the Mosque of Attarine on the site of Saint Athanasios'

Church, regularly visited by people attracted by the green-stone sarcophagus with the hieroglyphic inscriptions. It is curious how this sarcophagus from Memphis ended up in the centre of the city, and this could only have happened if Alexander had been placed inside for the journey from Memphis to Alexandria.

Following the discovery of the Rosetta Stone, deciphering the hieroglyphics became possible and proved, without doubt, that the green-stone sarcophagus was made for Nectanebo II, the last pharaoh, who had fled after the Persian occupation. The Rosetta Stone is of black basalt, and was found thirty-five miles (fifty-six kilometres) north-east of Alexandria by a Frenchman, Pierre Bouchard, in 1779. It is now in the British Museum in London. It was inscribed in two languages with three writing systems: ancient Egyptian hieroglyphics, demotic hieroglyphics and ancient Greek. The ancient Greek text was used as a base to make translation possible. Thomas Young began the task of deciphering, but the subsequent work was carried out by Jean-Francois Champollion, who established a complete list of hieroglyphic signs with their Greek language equivalents. In 1822, he published a scientific paper that allowed the future translation of all hieroglyphic texts, and made Egyptian writing on every subject accessible to the world.

In 1925, Evaristo Breccia excavated beneath the Mosque of Nabi Daniel but found no evidence of a tomb; therefore, the chapter concerning the burial of Alexander in that location must now be closed.

A new and interesting proposition in the search for Alexander's sarcophagus is that of Andrew Chugg. He has suggested that when, in 828 CE, Venetian merchants came to take the body of Saint Mark (their adopted patron saint) to their new cathedral in Venice, they had mistakenly taken the body of Alexander.

The history of Saint Mark varies considerably, but most versions agree that, in 68 CE, his body was mutilated by pagans. The Egyptian Orthodox Christians, known as Copts, maintain that the head of the saint had separated from the body, and they had preserved it for display whenever a new religious leader – the Coptic patriarch – was consecrated. Chugg's scenario is that, during the Christian rioting in 391 CE, Alexander's body could have been a target and a "good Samaritan" may have removed it from the tomb and reburied it in Saint Mark's Church for safekeeping, hoping that no one would search there for the body of Alexander the Great.

The Venetian merchants knew that the body of Saint Mark was in the church, so they took the coffin and packed it in a boat amongst pickled pork meat, in case Arab soldiers searched the boat, knowing they would not touch an area containing pork because it was prohibited by their religion. It would be easy to prove or disprove this scenario by opening the marble tomb in Saint Mark's Basilica: if there are only bones, and no skull, then they have the genuine remains of Saint Mark; however, if it contains a mummified body, it would be that of Alexander.

In 1989, a Greek archaeologist, Liana Souvaltzi, claimed that she had discovered a Macedonian tomb in the Siwa Oasis, which she thought could have been that of Alexander. However, after several archaeologists studied the area extensively, the idea was disproved. Of course, it is unlikely that Ptolemy I would have buried his friend Alexander the Great in this remote oasis. His rightful place was in a spectacular tomb in the city centre, for visitors to admire and pay their respects.

For over two hundred years, archaeologists, historians and other "experts" have been randomly searching for Alexander's tomb in Alexandria and other parts of Egypt, without success. After so much frustration for so long, it is time to settle down and deal with the problem systematically, using all the modern technology available in the 21st century. If the tomb still exists, with or without his body, it must be possible to locate it, since we can now retrieve objects from the surface of the moon and other planets.

There are four questions that need to be answered, and we must remain focused on these issues in order to progress:

The first question – was Alexander buried in the city? From the evidence that the tomb was visited, the answer is yes. The early visitors were Julius Caesar in 48 BCE, Octavian in 30 BCE and Strabo in 24 BCE – Zenobios, in the early 2nd century CE, confirmed Strabo's writings. Later, Emperor Hadrian in visited in 130 CE, Caracalla in 215 CE and two bishops from Constantinople – the centre of Christianity – visited in 325 CE.

The second question – during the Christian riots of 391 CE, there was much destruction of pagan temples, so is it possible that Alexander could have been a target and his mummified body was destroyed?

The third question – is Alexander somewhere else? Could a "good Samaritan" have moved the body and buried him in a church, another ancient cemetery or taken him to Memphis in Upper Egypt?

The fourth question – where is the site of the tomb built by Ptolemy IV and visited by so many celebrities? If it was so easily accessible to visitors, then it must have been close to the palaces. It is now possible to explore underground using sophisticated equipment: ground-penetrating radar, thermal imaging and ultrasound that can detect objects and spaces below the surface to a great depth, without damaging the present densely-built areas in Alexandria.

The Franck Goddio underwater archaeological team found remains of Ptolemaic buildings at a depth of fourteen yards (twelve metres) off the coast of Alexandria and, hopefully, further exploration may give us more clues. If the tomb was built inland, a few hundred metres from the coast, then it will be found around the palace area south of the Silselah peninsula or further east, close to the Greek, Jewish and Italian cemeteries in the district of Chatby.

CHAPTER SIX

Alexandria the Great

*You take delight not in a city's seven
or seventy wonders but in the answer
it gives to a question of yours.*
Italo Calvino, *Invisible Cities*

Alexander selected a plot of land, opposite the island of Pharos, between the Mediterranean coast and Lake Mareotis to the south. His first project was to connect Pharos Island to the mainland for accessibility, and built a causeway that divided the sea into two harbours. The distance between Pharos Island and the coast was seven *stades* – one *stade* being two hundred metres – a total distance of 1,531 yards (1,400 metres). The causeway was aptly named Heptastadion ("seven *stades*").

The eastern harbour, used by the Ptolemies, was known as the "Grand Harbour". Close to the eastern reef was the "Royal Harbour" and, on the west, was the "Harbour of Good Return", used for commercial purposes. In the centre of the eastern harbour, close to the coast, was a small island named Antirhodos, where the Ptolemaic rulers built a royal palace. East of Antirhodos, there was an elbow-like peninsula called Poseidon, where Mark Antony built a small sanctuary where he could rest and meditate after he lost the Battle of Actium to Octavian. He named the island Timonion, after Timon of Athens, a 5th century BCE recluse and contemporary of Socrates, who was disturbed by the ingratitude of the people. William Shakespeare wrote a play about Timon in 1623.

A spectacular lighthouse was built on the eastern tip of

the island of Pharos, near the Grand Library and Museum, west of the eastern harbour. Further to the southwest was a small fishing village, Rhakotis, which had existed for several thousand years and contained a temple dedicated to the Egyptian god Osiris. The area was connected with the Nile river through canals to Lake Mareotis, which made inland navigation possible. Greeks from the mainland and the Aegean islands traded with the Egyptians through the ports of Canopos, Menouthis and Thonis-Herakleion on the east, by the present Bay of Aboukir. These cities had been known for several centuries, well before the arrival of Alexander.

Herakleion was named after Herakles (Hercules), who came to Egypt to help during the Nile flood season. The city of Canopos was named after the steersman of the boat of King Menelaos. After the Trojan War, King Menelaos sailed to bring his wife, Helen of Troy, to his kingdom in Sparta but, due to bad weather, they lost their way and ended up on the island of Pharos. Studying the map, Troy and Alexandria are on the same longitude (30 degrees), so a north-westerly wind must have driven their boat from their planned route west to Sparta. They sheltered on the island for twenty days, until the weather improved. Canopos died from a snake bite and, for some unexplained reason, the Egyptians named the town, west of the Nile delta, after him. He also attained semi-divinity as a water carrier. The Franck Goddio underwater archaeological researchers found a bust of the water carrier, in the shape of a pot, lying submerged off the coast of Alexandria.

Ptolemy I, son of Lagos, started the Ptolemaic dynasty and made Alexandria the capital of the Greek Ptolemies. He, too, had an excellent education with Alexander under Aristotle, and wanted a similar education for his son, Ptolemy II. He invited Theophrastus, who was running the Lyceum in Athens after Aristotle's death, but he was too busy to leave Athens and recommended Strato of Lampsacos, a brilliant scholar with an extensive knowledge

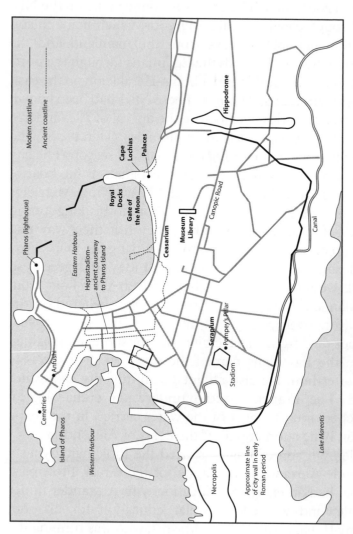

Ancient Alexandria's historical sites, with labels indicating monuments
by the eastern harbour and city centre.

of philosophy, biology and medicine, who tutored Ptolemy's son for six years.

Ptolemy conceived an idea to create a religious cult by fusing the Greek and Egyptian gods into one deity. For this difficult project, he needed the advice of Manetho, the Egyptian high priest and a scholar who had written books on the history of Egypt. Manetho guided him on how best to combine the gods in a way that was acceptable to the Egyptians.

Demetrios of Phaleron, the Athenian statesman, advised Ptolemy on how best to convince the Greeks. A decision was made to give the deity an Egyptian name – Serapis – melding Osiris (the god of the Underworld) and Apis, the Bull, who was the living representation of the god Ptah, creator of the universe. Ptolemy and Manetho designed a statue, with Hellenic features, of a robed, seated, bearded man; on his right knee sat the Egyptian three-headed dog of the Underworld and, in his left hand, he held the Asclepian wand of the healing god. To soften the image for the Greeks, they used the features of Zeus with a Dionysian expression to compensate for the negative image of the god of the Underworld, which was necessary for the Egyptians.

The Temple of Serapis was built in the village of Rhakotis, away from the religious administration of Memphis to the south. Alexandria, with the Serapeion, could now compete with all the other shrines in the ancient world. Ptolemy had achieved his ambition.

In 304 BCE, Ptolemy I took the title "King of Egypt", and was also named *Soter* ("the saviour"). He completed the city and port with a magnificent lighthouse, to illuminate and guide ships at night and to act as a fortress protecting the city. Ptolemy, by building the Museum and Grand Library, must have been aware that scientific knowledge brings power to a developing country.

Alexandria was developing into busy trading centre, and Ptolemy established a closed monetary zone for dealing with foreign merchants, who had to change their money into Ptolemaic gold, silver and bronze coins – silver being the most commonly used – while the bronze coins had a value of one-third of a silver tetradrachm. During the 3ʳᵈ century BCE, all gold jewellery was made by Greco–Macedonians, but the finest gold came from an area north of Sakkara, at the city of Tuch al Karamos.

The lighthouse and the ancient city

Ptolemy I conceived of the idea of a lighthouse as there was a hazardous stretch of water, studded with several long reefs, extending from the island of Pharos to the eastern tip of Cape Lochias. Sostratos of Knidos, an architect and mathematician of repute, designed a lighthouse that was so magnificent, it went well beyond Ptolemy's expectation. For the construction, he used limestone, granite and marble, reaching a height of approximately 120 yards (110 metres).

The first storey was a large, square building surrounded by a colonnaded courtyard, with more than two hundred rooms housing workers and mules, used to transport the wood for the fire by means of a double spiral staircase that ascended to the third storey.

Around the top of the first storey was a square platform, with a decorated cornice containing a Greek inscription: "Sostratos, son of Dexiphanes of Knidos, dedicated this to the saviour gods on behalf of all those who sail the seas." The "saviour gods" were meant to be King Ptolemy I and his wife, Berenice. On each corner of the platform were bronze tritons, mythological minor sea gods, that may also have been steam-driven foghorns to warn approaching ships.

The second storey was octagonal, with spiral ramps for transporting the wood logs (from tamarisk and acacia trees). The third storey was circular, with a very large reflector, where the fire was lit in the evening. The cover on the very top was an attractive conical structure and, one thousand years later, became a model for some mosque minarets. On the apex was a statue of Poseidon, made of polished brass, that rotated with the wind. Very little is known about the type of reflector on the third floor – whether it was made from polished brass, finely-wrought glass, or even possibly a lens designed by the Museum's scientists who worked on optics and telescopes.

It took twelve years to build the lighthouse, and was inaugurated by Ptolemy II (Philadelphus), taking the name of the island where it stood – Pharos. It was the symbol of Alexandria: a magnificent building, a technological masterpiece and one of the Seven Wonders of the World – and the only one of practical use. The construction was very solid; the first layer of the building was reinforced with molten lead, and stood for 1,500 years.

The architect Deinokrates constructed the city's roads based on the grid system attributed to Hippodamus of Miletos (on the eastern coast of Turkey), who was the first town planner in history. The grid system consisted of two wide main thoroughfares leading from north-to-south and east-to-west, with other smaller streets running parallel and dividing the city into sections, like a chess board. This allowed the fresh northerly winds to cool the citizens during the hot summer months. The thoroughfares were twenty-five metres (fifty-four feet) wide and lined with columns. People arriving at the port would enter Alexandria through the "Gate of the Moon" on the eastern harbour. The other entry to the city was from the east, through the desert via the "Gate of the Sun" and along the Canopic Road.

The area that housed the Museum and Grand Library, where most scholars and Greeks lived, was the "B" district (Brucheum). The Egyptians lived in the southwest district of Rhakotis, where the stadium and the Serapeion were built. The eastern district, "D" (Delta), was inhabited by Jews who came to Egypt around the 3rd century BCE.

Demetrios of Phaleron suggested to Ptolemy that it was necessary to translate the Hebrew scriptures into the Greek language. Ptolemy communicated this request to the high priest in Jerusalem, asking him to send seventy scholars who knew the Greek language to work on the translation. The scholars were provided with separate accommodations on the island of Pharos, so that they could be kept apart and not copy each other. After seventy-two days, the Hebrew translations into Greek were identical and perfect. This legendary translation of the Jewish books became known as the *Septuagint*, and was carried out for the benefit of the Greek-speaking world, as well as those of the Jewish diaspora who had a Greek education. The book was displayed in the Grand Library.

In 20 BCE, Philo Judeus, a Jewish theologian, started a school in Alexandria to explore the link between God and man, using *logos* ("the word") as a messenger. Alexandria had the largest Jewish population in the world, and they seemed to enjoy life, with abundant fresh water from the Nile, plentiful grain, cattle and poultry, and lived peacefully with the Egyptians and the Greeks – until the Romans invaded the city and began persecuting them.

The palaces, Museum and Grand Library

Palaces were built on the southern part of the peninsula of Cape Lochias (present-day Silselah), using different-coloured marbles that made the area very attractive. The architect had no knowledge that, a few thousand years before, all of this area had been covered by the sea, making it liable to subsidence – and this is exactly what happened in 393 CE and 1303 CE.

The royal palaces along the waterfront were built using

polychrome marble, granite, limestone and alabaster, with each subsequent ruler building his own palace using a different colour. These palaces must have looked stunning during the day and, at night, under a starry sky and a full moon, they would have glittered in the water.

The Museum, which incorporated the Grand Library, was built in the classic style using the same materials. In the early 1980s, archaeologists carrying out underwater exploration along the coast found several pieces of polychrome marble and granite, and two fine mosaics, submerged in the eastern port, that were most probably from the palaces.

The Museum had a large room, similar to an amphitheatre, with seats for meetings and lectures, called the Exedra, and several other rooms for research in mechanics and hydraulics, an observatory for astronomy and dissecting rooms for the study of animal and human anatomy.

The word "museum" is derived from the Greek word *mouseion* ("shrine of the Muses"). In mythology, the Muses were nine goddesses who were the patrons of arts and science. The function of the Grand Library was to be the storeroom of all knowledge, available under the guardianship of the Ptolemaic rulers.

Ptolemy I kept a diary throughout his life, recording the important events of Alexander's military campaigns. When he grew old, he appointed his son, Ptolemy II, as co-ruler, and used his leisure time to complete his memoir that, for centuries, was available in the Grand Library for everyone to read. Tragically, the book was lost, or destroyed in the fire of 48 BCE, but some other papyri from the diary survived and were used by Arrian (Arrianos), the Greek historian and Alexander's biographer. In the prologue of his book, Arrian said that he used Ptolemy's memoir believing that his information would be accurate and fair.

Ptolemy had a very successful life, creating the intellectual and glorious Alexandria, and died in his bed, in 282 BCE, surrounded by his family, at the age of eighty-four.

After his death, the Grand Library and lighthouse were completed by his son, Ptolemy II (Philadelphus), whose name means "friend of his sister".

The Ptolemaic rulers were responsible for appointing the librarians – a prestigious post. The first to be appointed, in 285 BCE, was Zenodotos of Ephesos, followed by the poet Apollonius of Rhodes; the mathematician Eratosthenes, from Kyrene (Libya); Aristophanes of Byzantium, who introduced accents into Greek writing; Apollonius of Alexandria; and Aristarchos of Samothraki. During their tenure, each of these librarians contributed something special that improved the function of the Grand Library.

The Grand Library was connected to the Museum by marble colonnades that were divided into numerous rooms, each one for a different subject, and where the papyrus scrolls were stacked in hollows in the walls or on shelves. These large rooms led into smaller ones, where scholars would take the scroll to stand and read, as there were no desks or seats. The complex of these two buildings was known as the "School of Alexandria" – the prototype of an academy or university. Surpassing the Academy of Plato and Lyceum of Aristotle in Athens, there was nothing like the Alexandrian Grand Library in the rest of the world. The first three Ptolemaic rulers funded the Museum and Grand Library, paid the scholars and provided them with accommodation. In the grounds of the Museum, there was a public walkway, a spacious park, botanical gardens and a zoo.

Another important area of the building was the communal dining room, where royals, scholars and students had their meals, talked, socialised and relaxed. Philadelphus was interested in science, and one can imagine him having lunch or dinner and discussing different subjects with Efklides (Euclid), the father of geometry; Sostratos, the architect of the lighthouse; Eratosthenes, the mathematician and global surveyor; or Herophilos, anatomist and physician.

Having researched the eating habits of Egyptians, Greeks and Macedonians, the author has devised a menu of three courses and a dessert that could have been served in the dining room. The meal starts with stewed fava beans served with slices of boiled egg, and morsels of chicken and duck on flat loaves of bread. The second dish is baked mackerel, which was abundant in the Mediterranean sea, split down the centre and filled with crumbled soft, white cheese and herbs. The main course could have been roast duck or pheasant, or quail in September, served with a date puree. A popular dessert in Alexandria was a cake, made from wheat and corn flour, covered with honey and sesame seeds. Wine was served in goblets, undiluted – a Macedonian habit, although the Athenians always diluted their wine with water to prevent inebriation.

The Alexandrians under the Ptolemies lived well; there was plenty of food as Egypt produced large amounts of grain, wheat, barley and a variety of vegetables. The staple diet of the Egyptians was, and still is, stewed fava beans served with oil or eggs, and this dish is still served as part of breakfast in hotels in Cairo and Alexandria. Cucumber was a pleasant, refreshing appetiser. Theophrastus the botanist suggested that, when dipped in milk, it becomes more succulent; today, the Greeks make cucumber parfait (known as *tzatziki*), using thinly-sliced cucumber and adding yogurt, a little garlic, a spoonful or two of virgin olive oil and finely-chopped mint or dill. There was plenty of fish from the sea and from the Nile, and they had various ways of cooking it. The Jews prepared mackerel by splitting it in half, packing it with salt and drying it in the sun. This has become a traditional dish in the Cycladic islands, and is known as *gouna*.

Red meat was plentiful – from buffalo, lamb and goat as well as chicken, duck and game. Ptolemy I, and others from Alexander's army who had fought and travelled in Asia, brought back fruits, nuts and spices not found in

Macedonia or Greece, and other interesting ingredients for the kitchen.

Ancient cookery books mention that the early Romans were "porridge-eating barbarians" because their bread was too soft, but the Greeks made firm bread from wheat and barley. The ancient Egyptians traditionally produced beer, but the Ptolemies preferred wine imported from Macedonia and the Aegean islands.

In Alexandria, there was plenty of entertainment. The ancient theatre on the hill performed plays by Greek tragic and comic playwrights. On the east, in the Jewish district, there was a racecourse, with sturdy, fast Thessalian and Egyptian stallions. There were also gymnasia, baths and a stadium for athletic games that took place after victorious battles or other celebrations. The Agora contained a very large square, where people would gather to meet friends and to talk, shop and sell their produce. It must have been wonderful place to spend a few hours during the day or early evening, on the coast surrounded by beautiful buildings.

Demetrios of Phaleron, pupil of Aristotle, philosopher and Athenian statesman, had left Greece for political reasons, and Ptolemy was lucky to have him. His advice regarding the Grand Library was invaluable, as he had previous experience spending time in Aristotle's library, which held a large and important collection. Ptolemy was anxious to collect as many books as possible, and Demetrios was given unlimited resources to purchase books – if a ship arrived with books, they would be bought or copied. The Grand Library started with two hundred thousand books and, within a short time, had reached a total of half a million, on subjects as diverse as literature, mathematics, astronomy, mechanics, medicine and cookery.

The material used for the books or scrolls was derived from papyrus: an aquatic plant with long stems, reaching a height of thirteen feet (four metres), that grew in abundance along the Nile river. The triangular stems were stretched into strips two inches (five centimetres) wide that were then pressed together and dried in the sun, with the glue-like sap of the plants acting as an adhesive. After further drying, the result was a thin writing surface, with the length of a standard papyrus being between twelve and sixteen inches (thirty to forty centimetres), with a width of four to eight inches (ten to twenty centimetres). Papyrus prepared in Alexandria was used for writing, mats and wrapping paper, and was exported all over the world. The Egyptians also used parchment and, like the ancient Athenians, pieces of ceramic called *ostraka*. Writing on papyrus or other materials also required the use of a reed or brush, and different colours of ink.

The librarians were highly educated, and a few were selected to act as tutors to the royal children. The first was Zenodotos of Ephesos, a grammarian and a man of literary distinction, who sorted the books according to their content: scientific or literary. The next logical step was to assign rooms, or part of a room, to the various categories of books, which were then arranged in alphabetical order by the name of the author. The poet Kallimachos of Kyrene made a great contribution to the Grand Library, without being an official librarian, by compiling the *Pinakes* ("Tables"): one hundred and twenty books containing a detailed biographical sketch of all writers. Eratosthenes, who served as the second librarian from 245 to 205 BCE, was the mathematician and geographer who measured the circumference of the earth.

For more than six hundred years, ancient Alexandria was the most fascinating city, architecturally beautiful, with two large ports, the lighthouse, Museum, Grand Library, stadium and "the greatest emporium in the inhabited world" – a city of gifts.

Literature, architecture and painting

There were many writers and poets who came to work and live in Alexandria after the completion of the Museum and Grand Library in 280 BCE. Several poets, hailing from all around the inhabited world, were attracted to the Grand Library; one worth mentioning is Sodates of Maronea, who devised his own poetic metre for satirical poems and invented the palindrome – where a sentence reads the same backwards and forwards. When Ptolemy II (Philadelphus) married his sister, Arsinoe, the Egyptians applauded the marriage but the Greeks considered it incestuous. Sodates is said to have written an obscene phrase in his poem and, accordingly, he met a bad end for offending his royal patron – he was encased in a coffin and thrown into the sea.

Ptolemy II encouraged many poets, particularly a group of seven who were known as the "Pleiads". Only the names of five are recorded, the most prominent being Lykophron of Chalkis, who was attracted to Alexandria and wrote a poem called *Alexandra* (or *Kassandra*) about the adversities of the Trojan War and its heroes.

The three great Alexandrian poets with extant works are: Theokritos, Kallimachos and Apollonius of Rhodes.

Theokritos moved from Sicily to Alexandria. His poems had a natural style, full of images, with a mixture of realism and love. He is known for his "idylls" (short poems), and became the father of pastoral poetry. Thirty of his poems have survived, and his work influenced both the poets of the Renaissance and the Britain of the 19th century. An example of a love poem concerns Simaetha, who was deserted by Delthis, her lover, and she tells her story to the moon for consolation:

Consider lady moon whence came my love,
I could have come by sweet love
As soon as it got dark

With two friends or with three
Carrying in my bosom apples of Dionysos
And on my head white poplar, the holy plant of Heracles,
Twisted all round with a crimson band.
(Translated by C. Trypanis, in *The Penguin Book of*
Greek Verse (1971)

Everyone knows that translating poetry is difficult, but I am convinced that this poem in English has more expression than when reading it in ancient or modern Greek.

Kallimachos, son of Battos, was born in the Ptolemaic colony of Kyrene (present-day eastern Libya) in 300 BCE, and moved to Alexandria, where he wrote both short and long poems of clear expression rather than emotion. He also wrote several historical poems as well as essays concerning the private lives of the Ptolemies. Of his six hundred volumes of poems, only one has survived. Kallimachos dedicated this short poem to the wife of Ptolemy III (Euergetes), and is titled *A Statue of Berenike*:

Translated by Peter Jay, in *The Greek Anthology*, published by Penguin Books (1973).

There are four Graces. Beside the original three
Stands one newly translated still dripping with scent
Blest and emulated by all, Berenike,
Without whom the graces themselves are not Graces.

Apollonius of Rhodes was born in Alexandria in 295 BCE. As a young man, he began an epic poem based on the story of Jason and the Argonauts in their quest for the Golden Fleece, written in Homeric style and entitled *Argonautika*. After a bitter quarrel with his teacher, Kallimachos, who disapproved of his epic poem, he left Alexandria and went to live on the island of Rhodes.

When Kallimachos died, Apollonius returned and was well received by the Ptolemaic ruler, who honoured him by appointing him as librarian. His book became a great success, as the Alexandrians loved it because of Jason's adventures on the voyage of *Argo* and his love affair with Medea.

Here are eight lines from book 1 of Apollonius' *Argonautika*, translated from the Greek, describing the strong rowing of the men in the *Argo* to the rhythm of Orpheos playing the lyre:

Exactly like young men who create a dance to honour Phoebos,
In Delphi or Delos or by the waters of Ismenos,
And all bring their quick feet down to the ground
Together around the altar
In time to the sound of the lyre
So they struck the turbulent sea with their oars to Orpheos' lyre
And the rushing waves surged up.
On either side the dark salt water broke into foam
Seething angrily at the might of such sturdy men.

The visionary Ptolemy I must have suggested to the architect, Deinokrates, that Alexandria should have a classic Greek style of architecture that blended with the larger monuments of the pharaohs, thus creating an evolution of larger-than-life and awe-inspiring buildings. However, despite their size, the buildings had Greek form and the principle of horizontal platform and entablature, comprising of a frieze and cornice supported by columns. Some of the edifices had two storeys with decorations, a vaulted roof, arch and copula, with the ground floor being Doric, the upper Ionic and the interior Corinthian. This same Hellenistic-style architecture also appeared in Pergamon and some other cities in Syria.

The Alexandrian school was not only about geometry, astronomy, geography, literature and medicine – it also bought about a change in painting techniques by intro-ducing detailed landscape art. For example, the landscape scenes from the *Odyssey*, exhibited in the Vatican Library, may not be exact reproductions of the Alexandrian painters but rather based on those from the Greek mural paintings in Herculeum. Most of the paintings in Pompeii, Rome and Campania were executed by Greek artists working in those cities.

After Octavian conquered Alexandria in 30 BCE, Greek artists went to Rome and painted pretty little figures, dancing girls, flowers and love gods. Another contribution was portraits using the "encaustic" method of heating coloured waxes on thin wooden panels. The wealthy had their dead mummified, and portraits were painted on the cover of the coffin or on a cloth. This technique was used in the 2nd and 3rd centuries CE, under Roman rule, and are known as "Fayum Portraits" after the town forty miles (sixty kilometres) south of Cairo, where the Hellenised inhabitants buried their dead. The portraits are lifelike images and very beautiful.

Alexandrian religious philosophy

During the three hundred years of the Greek Ptolemies, there were only a few philosophers, and none of their work has survived. The Alexandrians continued to study and pursue the works of Plato and Aristotle. With the gradual decline of the dynasty and the destruction of the Museum, teaching continued for a while in the Serapeion temple, and it was there that a new religious philosophy evolved.

In 220 CE, Ammonios Saccas, known as the founder of neoplatonism, started his own school of philosophy. Previously, he had been a porter in the dockyards (his Greek surname means "sack carrier") before giving up his job to devote his time to the study of Plato. Several pupils joined his school, the most important being Plotinos, who stayed with him for eleven years.

Plotinos was a Greek, born in Egypt in 205 CE, and conscientious, hard-working and logical. He decided to travel to learn about other religions, and the easiest and cheapest way to travel was to become a soldier. He joined the expedition to Persia by the Roman Emperor Gordian III. After the campaign failed in Antioch, he went to live in Rome, where he started a successful academy of philosophy. His lectures were described as thought provoking and stimulating, and explored the quest for a union of man with God. He described his own holy trinity, which starts with the "One" (meaning God), second is the "Nous" (the mind, or intellectual image of the "One"), and the third is the "Soul" (inferior to the "Nous", but the creator of all living things).

Plotinos began to write after the age of forty, recording his neoplatonic views. His most devoted pupil was Malchos, a Greek born in Syria who adopted the name of Porphyry. He became Plotinos' biographer, collected the fifty-four works of his teacher and edited them into nine books, the *Enneads*. For the first time in religious history, an Alexandrian had tried to solve the problem of linking God with man. Neoplatonism influenced early Christian theology and became the dominant philosophy in Europe for nearly a thousand years. Apart from the influence this had on Christians such as Saint Augustine and Boethius, some Islamic philosophers (Abu Nasr al Farabi and Ibn Sina Avicenna) and notable Jewish thinkers (Isaac ben Solomon Israel and Moses Maimonides), as well as British poets Shelley and Keats, were all influenced by neoplatonism.

The Ottoman invasion of Europe almost destroyed western civilisation. Christianity was the main pillar of intellectual activity, together with Greek philosophy and neoplatonism, all of which were important in removing the spectacle of ruin and misery to allow the contemplation of a world of goodness and beauty.

Science and scholars

From early times, Greeks in Ionia (Asia Minor) had been interested in the universe and mathematics, starting with Thales of Miletos, Anaximander and Demokritos of Abdera (in Thrace), and then by Pythagoras of Samos. Plato of Athens, in the first half of the 4th century BCE, was a mathematical visionary who famously said: "Knowledge of geometry is the knowledge of the eternal."

Around 300 BCE, something special happened in Alexandria that made mathematics the most important subject, followed by the sciences of mechanics, astronomy and cosmology. It may have started because of the presence of Euclid's school, which was eager to document geometrical figures and theorems from all around the world, and to publish them so they could be easily understood and accessible to all. This school was the first to realise that the universe could be better understood through numbers and geometry, and that no scientific progress could be made without a good knowledge of this subject.

On the subject of mathematics, one must start with the brilliant scholar Efklides (Euclid). Almost nothing is known of his personal life except that he worked in Alexandria between 300 and 260 BCE. He ran a school for clever students, and devoted himself to geometry, presenting the first account of a two-dimensional space in nature. He carried out extensive work on conics, optics and the study of curves, and progressed to the sciences of astronomy and navigation. His treatise was written on thirteen scrolls that are known as his *Elements*, which are innovative, logical, explicit and known to all mathematicians.

Euclidian geometry provided a concept of space in the physical world, presenting five geometric postulates, plus five additions known as the "common notions". The postulates freed the subject of geometry from guesswork and inaccuracy. Euclid was the first to demonstrate prime numbers, making him the "Father of Number Theory". His colleague in the Museum, Eratosthenes, described the simple "sieve method" to determine prime numbers. Euclid's *Elements* and Ptolemy's *Almagest*, on astronomy and geography, share the glory of being the world's longest-surviving scientific texts.

Apollonius of Perga (280–200 BCE) added new work on geometry and conic sections. Four of his books have survived in Greek, and three in Arabic.

Konon of Samos (280–220 BCE), astronomer and mathematician, was a teacher of Archimedes, with whom he shared knowledge for many years, even after Archimedes had returned to Sicily, as he often wrote to Konon when he solved difficult theorems.

Around 250 CE, Diophantos of Alexandria wrote the first treatise on algebra, mainly devoted to the solution of equations. He used symbolism in mathematics and is considered to be the "Father of Algebra". He shares this title with the Persian mathematician al Khwarizmi (780–850 CE), who published the first formula to solve quadratic equations and named the process *al Jabr* ("to solve"); therefore, the word "algebra" is derived from *al Jabr*. Six of Diophantos' books from his series *Arithmetica*, including works on number theory, were translated into Arabic and have survived.

From 300–200 BCE, the original works of Euclid, Archimedes and Apollonius of Perga ensured the continuation of geometry and mathematics – a unique scientific and cultural achievement.

The "golden era" ended after 200 BCE, and four-and-a-half centuries elapsed before Pappos of Alexandria (240–300 CE) advanced the study of mathematics by writing eight books – an important contribution to geometry and astronomy – and a few of his works have survived in Greek and Arabic.

Hypatia (355–415 CE), the first female mathematician, astronomer and philosopher, was taught by her father

Theon, who edited Euclid's books on geometry and worked on astronomy, making the texts easy to understand. As Hypatia's fame as a teacher spread, she had many students of all faiths, from the city and other countries including Libya, Syria and Constantinople. They all lived together as a close community based on Platonic thought. She may not have been a Christian, but neither was she a pagan, and was against violence and bigotry. Many of her students became important members of society, praising and admiring her for her truthfulness, high morals and modest style of dress and living. She adopted neoplatonism, which stated that, in man's search for God, one must give up the distractions of everyday life – which was similar to Christian teachings.

Alexandria was changing and, in 414 CE, Christianity was on the rise. After the death of Patriarch Theophilos, his nephew, Cyril, succeeded him. He was very ambitious and hungry for political power, and in constant conflict with the Roman prefect of the city. Hypatia had a reasonable relationship with both men but, because of her refusal to convert to Christianity, Cyril ordered a mob of Christians to kill her. This act of aggression by the early Christians, in 415 CE, was responsible for scholars fleeing from the city and a gradual decline in the reputation of the "School of Alexandria".

Applied mechanics

Archimedes (287–212 BCE) was born in Syracuse, Sicily, which was a colony of the Greek city of Corinth. History considers him to be the first real scientist. With an original and searching mind, he carried out experiments and utilised his theories for practical applications. It was the reputation of the Grand Library that first attracted him to Alexandria and, whilst he was studying there, he observed the rise and fall of the River Nile, designing the famous "Archimedian screw" that is still used in Egypt today, utilising modern materials but in its original form, to drain and irrigate fields.

Many scientific facts that we now know are from Archimedes' work: the sciences of mechanics and hydro-statics, the pressure of liquids at rest, the laws of levers and pulleys that led to machines that could move loads and change direction, the principles of buoyancy and the specific gravity of solids. Every schoolboy understands "Archimedes' principle" – that a floating or submerged body displaces its own weight of water.

Archimedes' work on mathematics is very extensive. He worked out the measurement of the total area of a circle, by multiplying the square of the radius with what is called the "Archimedian number" (pi), estimated at 3.142. He invented trigonometry, which relates distances to direction – essential for engineers and navigators – and laid the groundwork for calculus.

Archimedes returned to Syracuse to solve mathematical problems, and also began to develop defensive weapons to be used against the Romans who held Syracuse in siege. At the age of seventy-five, he was killed by a Roman soldier whilst sitting on a pavement in a street solving a problem. When Isaac Newton wrote "if I have seen further – it is by standing on the shoulders of giants" in 1675, he surely must have had Archimedes in mind!

No other people in the ancient world had shown such passion for mechanics and gadgets as did the Alexandrian Greeks.

Two extraordinary inventors were Ktesibios (285–222 BCE) and Heron, who lived during the 1st century CE. Ktesibios was the son of a barber in Alexandria and, as a young man, loved designing mechanical gadgets, using valves to ensure a flow of air and water. He was the pioneer of hydraulics, produced the first piston and cylinder – a prototype syringe then used to aspirate cysts – and, two thousand years later, this syringe was used for injecting fluids. He described the idea of using water power to push air, and used this concept to make a water-flute organ, from which the word "hydraulics" originates. Another invention was a water clock to measure the pulse rate (described in our later section on Alexandrian medicine). The design of the valve and pump led to the making of the first fire extinguisher. In our times, these discoveries would have been world-breaking news.

Heron, another ingenious engineer of the 1st century CE, noticed that steam produces power and is able to move objects, and sketched the prototype of a steam engine. In his book, *Pneumatics*, there are descriptions of various gadgets that the Alexandrians enjoyed, including a revolving model theatre, the first coin-operated machine (used to dispense "holy water"), a constant-volume dispenser for liquids and a large syringe used as a flamethrower.

Astronomers and geographers

Aristarchos of Samos (310–230 BCE) lived in Alexandria, where he founded the school of astronomy and was the first to propose the heliocentric theory, which states that the earth, the moon and other planets rotate around the sun. He studied the sizes and distances of the sun and the moon, and presented his findings in a short paper – his pioneering work in astronomy is still available today.

Eratosthenes was born in Kyrene (a Ptolemaic colony in present-day Libya) in 276 BCE. He used an ingenious method to measure the circumference of the earth: knowing that the earth is a sphere, he measured the angle of the shadows cast by the sun in both Alexandria and Aswan, five hundred miles (eight hundred kilometres) apart, on the same day in two successive years, and calculated the earth's circumference with an error of less than 10 percent. Another of his mathematical contributions was the simple "sieve method" used to find prime numbers. He was librarian of the Grand Library in 245 BCE.

Hipparchos of Rhodes (170–127 BCE), astronomer and mathematician, built the observatory in Alexandria and compiled the first catalogue of hundreds of stars, giving their positions in the celestial longitude and latitude. It is reported that he also calculated the distance between the moon and the earth.

Claudios Ptolemaios (known as Ptolemy) was born near Alexandria during the first part of the 2nd century CE. An astronomer, astrologer and geographer, he spent most of his time working and reading in the Grand Library. It is surprising that he was not influenced by the work of Aristarchos, adopting instead the geocentric theory that the universe revolved around the earth. This geocentric theory was also accepted by the Christian Church, delaying the science of cosmology for almost 1,500 years, until Nicholas Copernicus had the courage to publish his heliocentric theory in 1543 CE.

Ptolemy's major treatise on astronomy was called the *Almagest*: a series of thirteen books on such diverse subjects as "On the apparitions of the fixed stars", "On the planetary hypothesis", "Table of reigns" and "On Music". He also wrote the *Tetrabiblos* (a treatise on astrology), four books on optics and a selection of aphorisms that became popular titles. His *Almagest* was translated into Arabic and became the encyclopaedia of astronomy.

Astrology, according to Ptolemy, was prognostication through the basics of astronomy. His important contribution to the science of optics was noting that the refraction of light occurs on celestial bodies at various altitudes, which can create errors when observing the stars and planets. He wrote a guide to geography, *Geographia*, but with some errors, placing the equator too far north, extending Asia too far east and describing the Indian Ocean as bounded by a southern continent. Despite this, *Geographia* influenced explorers for centuries, and even Christopher Columbus used the book and its maps.

Another Alexandrian contribution is the calendar that we use today. Ptolemy III (Euergetes) drew attention to the existence of a leap day occurring every four years. The Egyptian priests issued a declaration stating that there should be three hundred and sixty-five and a quarter days in a year, but this was not adhered to. In 48 BCE, when Julius Caesar came to Egypt, he found the calendar confusing and consulted Sosigenes, a Greek astronomer, to find a solution. His suggestion was abandoning the lunar system and adding an extra day every four years. This system of calendar reckoning was named the Julian calendar and remained in use until 1582, when the Gregorian calendar was established, which is still used by most people today. The Muslims have retained their own calendar of a twelve-month year, with each month beginning at the time of the new moon; therefore, some months have twenty-eight days and others thirty days, and their year has either 354 or 355 days.

Alexandrian medicine

In his epic the *Iliad*, Homer reports that, during the Trojan War in the 12th century BCE, there were thirty-six head injuries – and all were fatal. There are records of the injured soldiers being moved from the battlefield to tents or nearby ships, where attention was paid to their wounds, cleaning them with warm water and applying soothing balms.

Around 430 BCE, a physician (writing under the name of Hippokrates of Kos) stated that disease had a physical cause rather than being a godly infliction – thus laying the foundations of rational medicine. He took careful notes of a patient's history, recorded the symptoms, carried out an examination, tried to make a diagnosis, advised treatment and reported on prognosis.

One hundred and twenty years later, two medical "giants" – Herophilos and Erasistratos –researched in the Museum, dissecting bodies of humans and animals, and practicing as physicians.

Herophilos of Chalcedon (335–220 BCE), who had been taught at Kos in the old Hippokratic school, carried out a detailed and meticulous dissection of human bodies and animals in the Museum. He found the connection between the brain and peripheral nerves, and was able to distinguish between motor and sensory systems. The anatomical dissection of the human liver, the duodenum that connects the stomach to the small intestine, and the male and female reproductive organs were accurately described. From the clinical point of view, he recognised the value of feeling the pulse to differentiate various types of heartbeat to diagnose heart problems – the pulse rate was measured using an automatic water clock, designed by Ktesibios who was working at the Museum. Herophilos was an accomplished physician, recognising that drugs are necessary to counter disease and that specific diets should be adhered to during illness.

Erasistratos (304–250 BCE) lived most of his life in Alexandria, and his most important contribution to medicine was his determination that the heart is a pump with valves. In simple words, the body is a machine and the heart is exactly the same as Ktesibios' water pump, designed with a set of valves controlling intake and regulating flow. When Erasistratos dissected the heart, he noticed membranes acting as one-way valves between the ventricles and the two main arteries, naming them the "biscupsid" and "tricuspid" (from the shape of an arrow point) – these names are still in use today. It was probably Erasistratos, or one of his pupils, who first successfully ligated a bleeding blood vessel, thus reducing mortality from haemorrhage after injury.

Erasistratos performed the first basal metabolism experiment, by studying a bird's intake of food and weighing its excreta. His outstanding and useful invention was the catheter, passed through the urethra to drain the urinary bladder at times of retention or in cases of renal haemorrhage. He is considered to be a pioneer of modern medicine.

When the Alexandrian Medical School was started by the British in the 1940s, the Egyptian authorities and medical staff honoured Herophilos by naming the anatomy lecture theatre after him, and the physiology room after Erasistratos. It is to be hoped that these names will not be changed because of modern political pressures.

Galen (Galinos, 130–101 CE) was born in Pergamon (a Greek city on the coast of Asia Minor), whose library was second only to that of Alexandria. He came to the city to study in the Grand Library and to research in the Museum, where he read, worked and wrote for nine years, and is remembered as the greatest physician of the ancient world.

His anatomical studies in the Museum led to the description of the cranial nerves and the sympathetic nervous system, while his study on the respiratory system and the mechanism of breathing had a positive effect on clinical work. Galen was a prolific writer of medical textbooks – twenty-two volumes survived to become the standard work in medicine for more than sixteen centuries. When Pergamon became a Roman city, the ancient Greek athletic stadium was converted to a gladiatorial arena and Galen was appointed as surgeon. After a few years, he went to Rome to practice medicine and, because of his competence and popularity, he was appointed physician to the court of Emperor Marcus Aurelius.

The Hellenistic scholars working in the Alexandrian Museum and Grand Library carried out research, taught and wrote extensively, and spread knowledge throughout the known world, laying the foundations of western science and creative thought.

When the Arabs conquered the Iberian Peninsula in 711 CE, they lived peacefully with an assortment of Christian minorities in the cities of Toledo, Granada and Cordoba.

They had in their possession Arabic translations of Ptolemy's *Almagest*, Galen's medical books, Euclid's *Elements*, as well as several of Aristotle's books, but none of them were available in Greek.

Francis Raymond de Sauvetat, Archbishop of Toledo from 1125–1152 CE, created a translation centre at Toledo, recruiting Arab, Greek, Jewish, Latin and Slav scholars to translate the important Greek works from Arabic. The translation centre carried on with this work until the 13th century CE. The West owes a debt of gratitude to both the Spanish church and the Arab scholars who preserved those Greek texts.

CHAPTER SEVEN

The Collapse of Ancient Alexandria

There are numerous incidents that contributed to the collapse of this magnificent city, starting with an accidental fire in the Grand Library that burnt hundreds of thousands of papyrus scrolls. This event was followed by the Roman invasion of 30 BCE, and sectarian conflicts related to the rise of Christianity, in 41 CE. The Roman leaders were concerned with the steady increase in the number of believers, and ordered the persecution of Christians and the destruction of their buildings. When the Christian Church was established, the opposite happened, and fanatical believers killed pagans and destroyed their temples. The rise of Islam brought about the Arab conquest of Alexandria in 641 CE. After all these invasions and sectarian conflicts that damaged the city, came the natural disasters: earthquakes, tsunamis and land subsidence.

In 48 BCE, Julius Caesar arrived in Alexandria for a visit after defeating his opponent, Pompey, at Pharsala in Greece. Cleopatra VII had been banished by her brother and his joint ruler, Ptolemy XIII, and she needed to speak to Caesar about her brother's unreliability, but this was proving difficult. By coincidence, a friend of Cleopatra – a Sicilian rug merchant – was in Alexandria to sell his wares. He cleverly smuggled her into Caesar's quarters in a bale of oriental carpets and, as he unrolled one of the rugs to display it, Cleopatra "popped out". It was rumoured that Caesar was instantly charmed and captivated by her.

Ptolemy XIII was displeased with the friendship

between Caesar and Cleopatra, and waged war on them. Caesar had arrived in Alexandria with a small army, thinking that, as a friend and an ally, he had nothing to fear. He became concerned with Ptolemy's aggression towards him and, when the fighting began, in order not to be trapped and be unable to escape, he used a diversionary tactic and set fire to the Ptolemaic boats in the harbour. Unfortunately, it was a very windy day and the fire spread quickly, causing damage to the Grand Library and Museum, and it is recorded that thousands of scrolls were burnt.

Caesar's reinforcements came quickly from a nearby Roman province, and were able to fight back. Ptolemy XIII realised that he was in danger of being captured and jumped into an overloaded boat to escape; but, as it moved into deeper waters, it sank – and Ptolemy drowned.

Caesar called on Cleopatra to rule Egypt with her younger brother, Ptolemy XIV, as consul. Caesar and Cleopatra formed a close relationship, especially as the queen spoke Latin and Greek. Knowing Caesar's interest in history, she organised a Nile river trip to show him the antiquities of Upper Egypt, Luxor, Karnak and Aswan. She soon had the most powerful man in the world under her spell and, during the trip, she became pregnant, giving birth to a boy in 47 BCE, and naming him Caesarion.

After three years, Caesar was assassinated by his "honourable friends" in Rome. His devoted general, Mark Antony, followed the fleeing perpetrators to Greece and defeated them at the Battle of Philippi, near modern Kavala in northeast Greece. Mark Anthony was keen to divide the Roman empire into two: Octavian (Caesar's nephew) would rule the West, and he the East.

Mark Antony spent the winter of 41–40 BCE in Alexandria, to meet Cleopatra and discuss a partnership for peace and prosperity. As a result of this relationship, she gave birth to twins – a boy and a girl. He then travelled around the East for four years, organising the provinces. During this time, Cleopatra was busy improving Egypt's economy by exporting vast amounts of grain to Europe, reorganising the army and increasing the navy by building more boats. When Mark Anthony returned to renew the relationship, they got married – despite the fact that he was still betrothed to Octavia, sister of the ruler of Rome. Mark Antony was impressed with the way that Cleopatra ruled her country, and crowned her and her son Caesarion as joint rulers of Egypt and Cyprus. The conquered lands in parts of the East were distributed to the three children of their marriage, showing how much he enjoyed sharing his eastern empire with her.

He brought books from Pergamon to replenish those in the Grand Library that were destroyed by the fire, and created a smaller one in the Serapeion temple, naming it the "daughter library". Although Cleopatra appeared to be a seductress, having an affair with Julius Caesar and then marrying Mark Antony, her aim was always to protect Alexandria from becoming a province of Rome.

Octavian was furious at the happenings in Alexandria, considering Mark Antony a traitor for distributing land to the children he had with Cleopatra and leaving his wife behind in Rome, and had no difficulty in convincing the Senate to declare war on Egypt. He sailed to the northwest coast of Greece, placing a huge army on the hills by the coast and deploying a large fleet of small boats that could be manoeuvred quickly. He waited for Mark Anthony at Actium (by present-day Preveza), where the naval battle took place. Mark Antony was badly prepared, having arrived with large ships that were difficult to operate, and he lost many men and vessels during the battle.

Cleopatra arrived with her navy and moored her ships further north, in a narrow stretch of water known as "Cleopatra's Canal" but, when she witnessed Mark Antony's desperate position, she panicked and turned her

ships around to return to Alexandria. Mark Antony had no
choice but to retreat and follow Cleopatra back to Egypt.

I could not understand why Mark Anthony, an experienced general who knew the area of northern Greece well,
could lose the battle so quickly, so I decided to visit the area
and see for myself. It is very lush and green, and the many
canals and small waterways that lead off the sea make it easy
to hide and manoeuvre the small boats that Octavian had
brought with him.

After Octavian's victory at Actium, it was easy for the
Romans to invade Alexandria. The final battle took place in
an area (now called Camp Caesar) where, seventeen
centuries later, coincidentally, most Italians lived from 1860
until the Egyptian military revolution of 1952.

Knowing that Octavian would treat them harshly, Mark
Antony and Cleopatra ended their lives in a personal way –
he, a soldier, with the sword, and she, having a fascination
with snakes, with a poisonous cobra. After three thousand
years of Egyptian civilisation, and three hundred years of
Ptolemaic Greek dynasties, Egypt became a Roman
province.

Cleopatra's legacy was the preservation of the Ptolemaic
dynasty for as long as possible, for which she struggled hard,
caring genuinely about her people. She used her intelligence, strong character, diplomacy and sex appeal to keep
Rome away from Egypt. Cleopatra was not beautiful, yet
she succeeded in luring powerful men. Blaise Pascal, a
French "man of letters", speculated that "if Cleopatra's
nose had been shorter, the whole face of the world would
have been changed."

When the Romans occupied the city, they continued
looking after the Grand Library and the Museum – the
"School of Alexandria" – but they were not particularly
interested in science. The majority of Romans did not speak
or write Greek, so the intellectual status of the city declined.
Octavian, on the other hand, was fascinated by the land-

scape and beautiful architecture of Alexandria, and converted Cleopatra's temple, the Caesarion, for his own use.

Christianity reached the city with the arrival of Mark the Apostle in 45 CE, and many Greeks and Egyptians were among his first converts. A church was built south of Cape Lochias, by the eastern port. The pagan Romans persecuted both Christians and Jews, killing hundreds, but failed to subdue the rapidly-increasing Christian movement.

In 215 CE, the Roman Emperor Caracalla, obsessed with Alexander the Great, visited his tomb but, on hearing that the young people of the city were critical of him, he ordered the slaughter of young men and the burning of parts of the city. In 251 CE, Diocletian's troops damaged buildings, palaces and temples; seventy years later, insurgents from Syria destroyed the Museum and Grand Library. In 365 CE, a tsunami hit Cape Lochias and the eastern coast of Alexandria, destroying royal palaces. The Institute of European Underwater Archaeology (IEASM) found large pieces of land, about 0.6 miles (one kilometre) off the coast, 4.4 yards (four metres) underwater as a result of land subsidence.

In 391 CE, although Christianity was still on the increase, violence broke out and Christians started killing pagans. A Christian mob destroyed the Serapeion that housed the "daughter library". Later, they partly destroyed the temple of Cleopatra, which was so well decorated and impressive that, although badly damaged by this attack, it attracted the attention of Constantine the Great from Byzantium, who restored the building and converted it into a cathedral dedicated to Saint Michael. It was in this church that Hypatia, the female mathematician and neoplatonist, was killed in 415 CE by a Christian mob.

When the Crusaders entered Alexandria in the 15th century CE, the only structure they saw standing was a pillar of red granite with hieroglyphics, known as "Pompey's pillar" – although it had nothing to do with Pompey, having been erected by the Romans for their Emperor Diocletian, who was mostly responsible for the destruction of the magnificent city.

Western historians have stained Alexander's reputation, calling him destructive, but the worst offenders were the Romans and the Christians. Around that period, a Christian question preoccupied the Alexandrians: whether Christ had one or two natures. The difference of opinion was whether the two natures had remained independent or had become fused into one nature – monophysitic.

The debate started with two Alexandrian prelates with opposing views – Arios and Athanasios. Arios was a senior priest who maintained that the Son (meaning Christ) was not equal to his Father, whereas Athanasios, a theologian and deacon, took the view that Father and Son were equal, formed of the same substance but distinct divinities. The Arian doctrine was embraced by a few theologians in Byzantium, the Greek city on the shores of the Bosphorus that later became the capital of the eastern Christian empire. The view of Athanasios, that Father and Son were equal, was accepted by the majority. However, Emperor Constantine, ruler of Byzantium and a recent Christian convert, was concerned that these two different views might damage the progress of Christianity, and felt it necessary to have the Church united. He organised a meeting of the hierarchy to decide which doctrine should be accepted. At the Court of Nicaea, near the Black Sea, attended by 250 bishops, deacons and priests, a decision was made, by an overwhelming majority, to reject the Arian doctrine.

Athanasios returned victorious to Alexandria, with the authority of Nicaean orthodoxy behind him and, at the age of thirty-three, became patriarch of Alexandria in 328 CE. The ruler in Byzantium declared that, although Arios was a heretic, he should be allowed to return and live in Alexandria, but the patriarch refused. The authorities also accused Athanasios of mismanagement, and exiled him. When he was very old, Athanasios returned to Alexandria to live until his death – in 373 CE, he became venerated as a saint.

The Christians who continued to believe in one nature – the "monophysites" – were the Copts (the name comes from an adaptation of the Greek word for "Egyptian"), who formed a separate community and remain true to their belief today.

Alexandria and Byzantium (later Constantinople, present-day Istanbul) were in regular conflict over Christian doctrinal issues, which meant that they did not cooperate militarily and Alexandria received no support from Byzantium, leaving its defences weak and making it easy for Arab invaders to conquer the city.

With the decline of Roman power in the East and a weakening of the leadership of Byzantium, the Arabs were gaining popularity in neighbouring countries, where thousands of people were converting to Islam. Amr Ibn al As, an Arab soldier who had converted to Islam, seized Palestine and carried on to conquer Egypt. He defeated the Christian forces at Heliopolis, by the Nile delta, and founded another city – Fustat, near present-day Cairo. In 641 CE, he marched into Alexandria from the east, through the "Gate of the Sun", hoisting Mohammed's banner above the walls of the city. Reportedly, he was amazed when he saw the city, and over-exaggerated by telling his caliph that Alexandria contained "four thousand palaces, four thousand baths, four hundred theatres, one thousand greengrocers, and forty thousand Jews". Scholars do not agree with the four thousand palaces and baths, of course, but do agree that there were thousands of greengrocers and Jews. The Arabs were full of praise for the city and did not inflict any further structural damage to its buildings.

In 700 CE, the lighthouse was still functioning. After a minor earthquake, the lantern fell to the ground; in 1200 CE, a stronger earthquake caused the second storey to collapse; and in 1303 CE, a tsunami shook the entire peninsula and eastern coast – and everything sank into the sea.

Franck Goddio, founder and director of the IEASM, working in collaboration with the Supreme Council of Egyptian Antiquities and the Oxford Centre of Marine Archaeology, has carried out underwater exploration around the eastern harbour and Bay of Aboukir – with spectacular findings. With continued underwater exploration, new findings may shed light as to the whereabouts of the Ptolemaic monuments, and answer the question of whether they were submerged in the sea by natural disasters or were destroyed by invaders.

CHAPTER EIGHT

The Rebirth of Alexandria 1,400 years After the Collapse of the Ancient City

In 1517 CE, the Ottomans defeated the Mamelukes and occupied Egypt for almost three hundred years. They governed the country from Constantinople, and used the port of Alexandria for transport of grain and other exports. They were unconcerned with the city, only anxious to keep the agriculture at a high level of productivity, and the no-longer-famed Alexandria was so neglected that, by the 19th century CE, the tributary that brought water from the west branch of the Nile had silted up, reducing the water supply, and the local population was reduced to a few thousand.

Napoleon Bonaparte's conquest of Egypt, in early 1798, was intended to prevent the British from increasing their domination of the East. His initial naval success was to sneak past Nelson's fleet and occupy the Bay of Aboukir, east of Alexandria. The French forces pushed the Turkish soldiers back, reassuring the native Egyptians of their good intentions and respect for their civilisation. Napoleon, knowing that he would be occupying Egypt, brought with him more than a hundred *savants* (scholars and scientists) to study the ancient Egyptian civilisation.

When he moved to Alexandria, he must have been surprised that the city and port, once known for its lighthouse, Museum, Grand Library, palaces and temples – all of which had disappeared – had been reduced to a village, and the Pharos peninsula had become a poor Turkish district.

On 1 August 1798, Horatio Nelson, admiral of the British navy, carried out a surprise attack that destroyed the entire French fleet. Napoleon was faced with two problems: he was cut off from the sea, and the Egyptians were hostile to the presence of the French army in the towns and villages – Napoleon's "hand of friendship" had not been accepted. Two years after the defeat of the French fleet, the British moved inland and fought against the remaining French troops. Napoleon realised that his presence was not sustainable, abandoned his ambition and left Egypt.

Although the French stayed for only two years in Egypt, their cultural influence was impressive and lasting. They discovered the Rosetta Stone, which led to the deciphering of hieroglyphics, and the "lingua franca" in Egypt remained French until 1950. Streets were named *rue* and the squares were called *place*, and they also left behind schools and other cultural institutions.

The British, having defeated the French troops, decided not to prolong their stay in Egypt and soon left. The Ottoman sultan appointed Mohamed Ali to protect the country from western insurgents. Ali was born in Kavala, in northeast Greece. He was of Albanian descent, intelligent and shrewd, and had proved a promising and competent soldier in the Turkish army, having liberated the Arabian Islamic holy places of Mecca and Medina from the Wahhabi Muslims – a heretical sect who were a nuisance to the Ottomans.

In 1807, the British government, knowing that Mohammed Ali's ambition to dominate the East would consequently lead to their loss of access to Asia via Sinai to the Red Sea, became hostile to the Ottomans. Using well-prepared troops, they took control of the port of Alexandria and the eastern territories by the Red Sea. However, Mohammed Ali had anticipated this move and soon defeated the invaders, capturing half of the British troops. Both sides were willing to negotiate, and Mohammed Ali agreed to release the British prisoners in exchange for the withdrawal of all British troops from Egypt. This victory over Britain made Mohammed Ali confident and powerful. He laid out a programme for the modernisation of the city based on western lines, deciding to make Alexandria his capital, and had ambitious ideas for the port to be transformed into the trading centre of the Mediterranean.

Ali reopened access to water from the western branch of the Nile delta by cutting out a forty-five mile (seventy-three kilometre) canal, named Mahmoudieh. This project was successfully completed by 1820 and, with plenty of water available, he started his construction programme.

The British and Europeans were encouraged to come to the city, and were offered special concessions in return for making Alexandria prosperous. When Mohammed Ali took over in 1805, the foreign expatriate population did not exceed one hundred – by 1830, there were more than five thousand. Domestically, he imposed heavy taxation on the landowners, which many could not afford; in a relatively short period, he had become the largest landowner in the area, gaining control over the production of grain and other crops.

The ancient Egyptians did not know anything about cotton, and had used flax to make their clothes. Ali was stimulated by a Frenchman who had cultivated several acres of land with cotton. During his younger years in northern Greece, he had met Michael Tositsas, a successful businessman, and asked him to join him in Egypt to begin cotton cultivation.

In 1821, coincidentally, Theodore Koloktronis (army chieftain of the Greek freedom fighters) rose against the Ottomans, defeating thirty thousand of their troops at the Battle of Dervenakia. This was the first successful campaign against occupiers of Greece for four hundred years, and alerted the western world to help the Greeks liberate their country from the Turks. On the orders of the Ottoman sultan, Ali sent a large Egyptian army and fleet, under the command of his stepson, Ibrahim, to reinforce the Turks fighting in southern Greece. The Alexandrian Greeks were shocked that Ali, who had pretended to be a friend of Greece, had taken this action. Fortunately, Britain, France and Russia took notice, finding this Egyptian military support of the Turks unacceptable, and sent ships and troops, defeating the Ottoman and Egyptian forces at the Battle of Navarino in southwest Greece. Lord Byron was responsible for arousing philhellenic feelings in Britain, through his autobiographical poem *Childe Harold's Pilgrimage*, published in 1812. Here are three stimulating lines from Canto II, on the revival of the Greeks:

> *With thy unquenched beam, lost Liberty!*
> *And many dream that the hour withal is nigh*
> *That gives them back their father's heritage.*

From his poem *Don Juan* (1820), "The Isles of Greece" became the most important philhellenic stanza:

> *And musing there an hour alone*
> *I dreamt that Greece might still be free.*

Cotton production in Alexandria had started in 1820; by 1840, the industry was booming and the city had become the major exporter of cotton to Europe. Twenty years of civil war in the United States had diminished their export of cotton to Europe, and Egypt had benefited.

A practical move by Mohammed Ali was to give free land around the main city square, named *La Place des Consuls* by the French, to foreigners in order to build churches, synagogues, consulates and commercial offices. On the southeast of the square was the cotton and stock exchange,

"The Bourse", the city's most important landmark. On the other side of the square, the French Gardens and the Anglican Church of Saint Mark were located.

After Mohammed Ali's death in 1849, he was succeeded by his eldest nephew, Abbas I, who granted the British a concession to build a railway line from Alexandria to Cairo, with an extension to the Red Sea. Abbas was followed by Said Pasha, son of Mohammed Ali, who returned the land taken from the farmers by his father, but his most important decision was the granting of permission to a French engineer, Ferdinand de Lesseps, to construct a canal connecting the Mediterranean to the Red Sea.

The ruler who did most to modernise Egypt, and was genuinely pro-European, was Khedive Ismail, grandson of Mohammed Ali, who had inherited the qualities of leadership and dynamism from his grandfather. Some of his progressive legislation was to abolish slavery and to encourage farmers to cultivate their land without paying tax. He started postal and telegraphic services, invested in military schools, and allowed mixed tribunals to operate in Alexandria. He built up the railway system and improved the docks, but his largest project was overseeing the completion of the Suez Canal. To celebrate this important event, Khedive Ismail organised a sumptuous inauguration in 1869, with Princess Eugenie, the wife of Napoleon III of France, as his guest of honour. He commissioned the composer Guissepe Verdi to write an opera with an Egyptian theme – *Aida* – to celebrate the occasion; two years later, its premiere was held at the new Opera House in Cairo, and it is still one of the most popular operas today.

Under Khedive Ismail, urban development was impressive – especially in the eastern suburbs, where many mansions and villas were built in various European styles. The hub of the city was the square named after Mohammed Ali, and a large bronze statue was erected in his honour in 1872.

Egypt's economy was deteriorating. Ismail was a spend-thrift because of the modernisation programme, and there were many financial problems. The only way that he could deal with the country's debts was to sell 177,000 Suez Canal shares, worth four million pounds, to the British government during Disraeli's premiership. The sale of the shares meant that Egypt no longer had any rights over the canal company, and the British and French became the sole owners. As there were other substantial debts, pressure was applied on the sultan by western leaders and banks to depose Ismail and, unfortunately for Egypt, he was exiled to Istanbul in 1879. Surprisingly, it was his "friends" – the British and French politicians who had supported him and nicknamed him "Ismail the Magnificent" – who were responsible for his downfall. Instead of helping out with the debt, as would happen these days with successful leaders, they got rid of him!

It was after the exile of Khedive Ismail that the British became more politically involved with the country, resulting in a flare-up of nationalism. In 1882, Ahmed al Orabi, the minister of war, started an uprising against foreign interference and the despotism of the ruler Khedive Tawfiq, which sparked violence – more than one hundred Christians were killed. This reaction alarmed the Europeans, and twenty thousand of them left the city. A few months later, Great Britain, under pressure by the foreign communities to suppress Egyptian nationalism, bombarded the city and succeeded in defeating al Orabi, but caused much structural damage.

After Egypt's declaration of independence in February 1922, and a century of Khedive and Pasha rule, it was decided to change to a monarchy. Fuad I, seventh son of Khedive Ismail, was crowned king. He was not an effective monarch, having persistent problems with the political parties and their members. After Fuad's death in 1936, his son, Farouk, became king at the age of eighteen. He was very young, gentle, and a new hope for the people but, with the passage of time, people became disappointed at his extravagant lifestyle and the unnecessary war with Israel that led to an embarrassing defeat.

He divorced his first wife, Queen Farida, who had produced three daughters but no male heir, and married a commoner, Nariman, who bore him a son. Before the start of the Second World War, King Farouk was pro-Nazi, hoping that the Germans would free Egypt from western dominance. The Allied forces put pressure on the king and his ministers to change their mind and, in 1940, Egypt declared war on Germany.

Before and during the Second World War, the city centre was always busy: the electric trams to the eastern suburbs were packed with people, and the restaurants, dancing clubs and cinemas were full to capacity. Further east, the popular beach resorts of Stanley Bay and San Stefano were crammed with hotels and restaurants open in the evenings for dinner and dance. At weekends, these beaches were popular with both young and old, enjoying themselves under the clear Alexandrian sky and swimming in the warm sea.

After San Stefano, the next tram station was Laurens, where my parents and most of my Coptic, Egyptian and Jewish friends lived. It had been named after a French cigarette manufacturer who had built a small, attractive palace called the Hermitage. Parallel to the tram station, on the coastal road, was the Swiss-owned Hotel Beau Rivage, with its private beach and an attractive, well-planted garden, serving meals throughout the day. High Tea in the afternoon – this was one of our favourite meeting places.

The next resort was Sidi Bishr, considered the most fashionable in Alexandria, which had three excellent beaches with fine gold sand and was always clean. There were wooden cabins on three tiers of promenade, each with its own veranda, consisting of a single room where we could change into our bathing costumes and store our clothes, with wooden chairs provided for use on the veranda. The cabin we used was owned by two close friends, the Bishay brothers. During the weekends in the summer months, we spent mornings on the beach, riding the waves on flat boards, swimming and playing rackets. As it was not allowed to stay on the beach or in the cabin after sunset, a group of friends rented a chalet across the road from the beach, where we had parties in the evenings and, on Sundays, our girlfriends would cook at home and bring tasty dishes for lunch or dinner.

At Victoria College, my close friend was Cherif, an Egyptian who was a neighbour living on a parallel road. His villa was in lush grounds of ten acres, with lawns and mature trees. In the grounds, away from the villa, there was a separate two-storey house where Cherif and his sister lived, being looked after by a maid and a German governess. His maternal relatives were ministers in the government and had close connections with the royal family – it was rumoured that Cherif could be the choice of one of the princesses. As most of our friends were keen on football, we played five-a-side on his lawns, and mixed matches with girls. We both liked British and American films and, on Saturday afternoons, were chauffeur-driven into the city centre to one of the several cinemas. The memories of my school and university days, the parties in our cabin and the friendship with Muslims, Jews and Greeks, are still vivid in my thoughts.

In summary, the founder of the modern city was Mohammed Ali – a visionary who was aware that, with multi-ethnic support and guidance, Alexandria could develop and prosper, and the two cultural influences would make life pleasant, safe and interesting for all its citizens. Tourists, scholars and artists were attracted to Alexandria, the locals were polite with a good sense of humour and everyday dealings with people were honest. The European-style city on the Egyptian shore – *Alexandria ad Egyptum* – was an enviable place for all of us to live.

CHAPTER NINE

The Foreign Communities
The People and their Contribution

The founders of ancient and modern Alexandria were multi-ethnic, including scholars, scientists and businessmen – only the workers were Egyptian. After Alexander's death in 323 BCE, Ptolemy Lagos (a Macedonian Greek), instead of returning to his home, went to Egypt to build a city at the site that Alexander had chosen. He befriended the Egyptians, explained his plans to them and started work on several projects. His aims were the construction of a port with a lighthouse – the first in the ancient world – the building of a museum and library to become a centre of learning, with the emphasis on science, and the creation of a shrine to fuse the Greek and Egyptian gods into one deity. Ptolemy encouraged immigrants from mainland Greece, the Aegean islands, Asia Minor, Judea and Ethiopia, as well as Egyptians from Upper Egypt. The rulers were the Ptolemies, the culture Hellenistic and the military Macedonian. Within twenty years, the city was known as the "School of Alexandria", specialising in geometry, mathematics, mechanics, medicine, literature and religious philosophy.

Alexandria had the largest granary in the ancient world and, with the presence of a very large harbour and lighthouse facilitating the export of grain and many other commodities, had the potential to become the "greatest emporium of the known world". During the reign of Ptolemy I, the population of Alexandria was between eighty and one hundred thousand, with Egyptians, Greeks, Jews and others all working together in peace, but living in separate districts.

Ptolemy started the dynasty and, over the next three hundred years, there were seventeen rulers before the Romans invaded the city in 30 BCE, when Octavian occupied Alexandria and Queen Cleopatra VII, the last Ptolemaic ruler, committed suicide.

In 1805, Mohammed Ali was appointed governor of Alexandria. He, too, was not a native, being born in Kavala (northern Greece), was of Albanian descent and a serving officer in the Turkish army. When he arrived, Alexandria had shrunk to the size of a village, but he realised that, by bringing water from the western branch of the Nile, he could create a populous commercial centre. In order to accomplish this task, he needed outside help – Europeans who were prepared to live, work and invest in Alexandria – attracting them by offering tax concessions and plots of land to build their own institutions, churches and synagogues. He also commissioned members of the foreign communities to help him develop the modern city. Gradually, the Europeans became partners in administrating the municipality and its affairs, both commercially and socially, being employed in various departments, including the police force, and all helped the city to become integrated – to the benefit of everyone.

From the 1840s onwards, the city flourished both financially and socially, with the British and Greeks being the cosmopolitan elite. In 1890, the British started the Sporting Club, which had horse racing twice a week, along with betting, plus areas for cricket and bowling. After the Second World War, they added tennis courts and invited renowned players from England and Australia for demonstrations, coaching and matches.

After Khedive Abbas Helmi II was deposed in 1914, Egypt became a British protectorate in the hope of curbing

Egyptian nationalism. However, in 1919, Saad Zaghloul (a nationalist leader living in Alexandria) started another revolution, which ended when he was exiled to Malta. During the next two years, there was constant pressure from British intellectuals and politicians to grant sovereignty to Egypt – and this they did in 1922.

Oswald Finney was one of the richest Englishmen abroad, inheriting the Alexandria Commercial Company from his father – a cotton export firm and the most successful in the East. He became the proprietor of all English and French newspapers and magazines in the area. Other prominent British names were the Barker, Carver, Moss and Peel families, all successful in shipping and commerce. The annual masked ball, organised by the Finney family and held in the ballroom of their five-storey house, was one of the highlights of the year. The British supported several charities, and subsidised theatre and opera performances in the city where they enjoyed living.

By 1920, new varieties of high-quality cotton had been developed and exports were revitalised. The cotton was divided into the long-staple *karnak* and *menoufi* types, and the medium and short *ashmouni*, *giza* and *zagora* (names given by the British and Greeks to the high-quality varieties). They also pioneered the use of the first steam-powered ginning machine, manufactured in Oldham, England, that separated the cotton from the seed.

From 1936, during the reign of King Farouk, Alexandria was the home of deposed royal families from the Balkans. These exiled families mixed very well with the British – to the extent that Prince Nicolas Petrovitch of the Romanov family had good times at parties with writer Laurence Durrell.

During that decade, the British government appointed a professional diplomat, Sir Miles Lampson, as ambassador. He settled well in Egypt, taking it upon himself to look after the young king, then aged eighteen, and was determined to groom him to become an "English gentleman". Sir Miles supported Moustapha Nahas, the prime minister at the time and leader of the Wafd party, but Farouk took it upon himself to replace him with Mohammed Mahmoud, an Oxford-educated Egyptian, who immediately changed all the cabinet members. Sir Miles considered the event carefully, and found that many of those newly appointed were Italian fascists – and Mussolini was an ally of Hitler. He persuaded the young king that this action was unacceptable, and the previous cabinet was reinstated. At that time, the British had a good understanding of the country's internal affairs, and some political influence.

The Greek community – the largest in Alexandria – was hard-working and successful. They cultivated and improved the quality of cotton, and started the production of cooking oil from cotton seeds. Michael Tositsas was born in Metsovo, Epirus (in western Greece) and, in 1820, moved with his brother, Theodore, to Alexandria, where Mohammed Ali gave them land to cultivate cotton.

George Averoff was also born in Metsovo, and Tositsas asked him to join them in the city, where they both prospered. Averoff became a successful cotton merchant and purveyor of luxury goods to Khedive Ismail. Like Oswald Finney, he had inherited a large fortune and supported many charitable organisations, building several schools for the Greek community. He was also responsible for building the marble stadium for the modern Olympics in Athens, in 1896, and donated the first frigate to the Greek navy.

Michael Salvago, a cotton exporter, opened the Bank of Egypt, married the daughter of Emmanuel Benaki – a beautiful woman considered to be the *grande dame* of Alexandria – and lived in the east of the city, in "Quartier Grecque", along with other wealthy Greeks. Emmanuel's brother, Anthony Benaki, well educated and always stylishly dressed, entertained British and foreign celebrities in his impressive villa, the interior of which was decorated with Egyptian and Oriental pieces. The Benaki–Choremi cotton company was one of the first businesses in Egypt, and used its profits to built schools, an orphanage for the Greek community and helped the less well-off. In the 1940s, the Benaki family donated their antiques collection to the Greek state, which is now housed in museums in Athens.

In the mid-1800s, cigarette manufacturing was started by Armenians and Greeks, mixing Greek tobacco with other leaves. Annual production was eighty million cigarettes, of which 80 percent was exported. Sales in Alexandria rocketed during the First and Second World Wars, as the soldiers were heavy smokers!

There were three families who produced alcohol from molasses (a by-product of processing sugar cane) for industrial and medical use. The main producer, Theodore Kotsikas, used the profits to build a large, efficient, modern hospital.

It was during Mohammed Ali's rule that Sephardic Jews came to Alexandria. The first banker and businessman was Jacob Levy de Menasce, who opened a bank in Cairo and was financial adviser to Khedive Ismail. When he heard that the city on the Mediterranean coast was developing successfully, with cotton and exports, he moved his businesses to Alexandria. Within a few years, a commercial zone had been created in the city centre and the numerous banks were efficiently processing 94 percent of its export business.

His "empire" was passed onto his sons: Jacques de Menasce started railway manufacturing, and bought land for the production of sugar cane and cotton, while Felix took over the management of the banks. The highlights of the summer months were the Tuesday-afternoon concerts, where Felix's son, George – an accomplished pianist – entertained music lovers in the spacious garden of the family house on the corner of two roads (Menasce and Rasafa) in the district of Moharrem Bey. Their house was visited by

European celebrities, and regularly by Chaim Weizmann, president of the World Zionist Movement. Dr Weizmann and his Royal Highness Amir Faizal, representing the Arab kingdom of Hegaz, signed an agreement on 4 January 1919, the main article of which stated that: "Relations should be controlled by the most cordial goodwill and understanding, and to this end Arab and Jewish duly-accredited agents shall be established and maintained in their respective territories." Maybe, if this had been adhered to, the Middle East would be a different place today. Both signatories were sincere in wanting the best for their own countries and, in 1949, Weizmann became the first president of the State of Israel, supported financially by the Menasce and other Jewish families living in Alexandria.

Italians began to settle in Alexandria in the 1900s. They were mostly professional workers, skilled builders and technicians, responsible for designing the attractive buildings in the city. The architect Alessandro Loria was born in Mansoura, his father having emigrated from Tuscany. Loria was very talented, and designed the famous Cecil Hotel (presently the Sofitel), the Majestic, the Venetian-style Lido, the city's synagogue, the Italian hospital and the National Bank of Egypt with its mosaic decoration, as well as many apartment blocks and villas with attractive designs in multicoloured bricks.

The Italians started the first cinemas in 1897, projecting short films during theatre performances, and Barda converted the Egyptian Theatre into a cinema named "Olympia", which proved so popular that cigarette manufacturers and chocolate makers gave free tickets to customers who bought their products regularly.

In 1927, according to the first statistical population survey of Alexandria, there were 230,000 Egyptians, while the total number of foreigners residing in the city was 110,000: 36,000 were Greeks, 22,000 Italians, 20,000 Jews, 15,000 British and 9,000 French. By 1950, there were half a million Egyptians, 100,000 Greeks, 30,000 Italians, 30,000 Jews and 10,000 British.

Six thousand years ago, the ancient Egyptians in Upper Egypt had produced a beer made from barley and hops – and the modern Alexandrians revived this industry. The Greeks were the first, with their "Crown Brewery", and called their beer "Stella", which fast became their best-selling product. It was very popular with the Allied forces during the Second World War; a 1939 British film, *Ice Cold in Alex*, starring the young actor John Mills, portrayed British troops stationed at El Alamein looking forward to having a cold glass of beer in Alexandria after their tour of duty.

The foreign communities helped to modernise Egyptian agriculture by introducing new machinery for the cultivation and collection of grain, vegetables and fruits. Given the increasing foreign population, they built schools to educate their children, and cultural institutions and hospitals. The French had the "Mission Laique" governing the Lycee Francais (a mixed school), the Catholic Fathers ran Saint Mark's School for Boys, and Saint Catherine's College for Girls was successfully administered by nuns.

The Italians also started the Don Bosco Institute, with upper, lower and technical schools – the last of which was popular with other foreign communities.

There were five British schools, which were open to all nationalities: Saint Andrew's, the British Boys School, the Scottish School for Girls, the English Girls College, and Victoria College (a day school and boarding school for boys). Victoria College had been created to educate the sons of the British living and working in Egypt and, later, taught the sons of the rulers of emerging petrol-producing countries, such as Saudi Arabia and the Arab Emirates. Prince Faizal of Iraq and Prince Hussein of Jordan became pupils at the school, and the sons of exiled Balkan royal families – Simeon of Bulgaria, Zogo of Albania, Constantine of

Greece and the grandson of Victor Emmanuel of Italy – were all schoolmates at Victoria College, seeking the best education available in the Middle East.

The electric tram route ended at Victoria Station, behind the school. Seventy acres of land had been purchased by George Anderson in the area of Siouf, chosen for the school because it was an attractive "oasis". The architect, Henry Gorra, used Italian renaissance architecture (popular in Victorian Britain), joining the two main buildings together with a long hallway, the dining room leading off from it, and adding a central clock tower and a Moorish façade.

The upper- and lower-school buildings faced green fields, where football was played in the winter and cricket in the summer months. There were a total of five hundred pupils in the upper and lower schools, with more boarders than day boys. At the age of eleven, my father moved me from a Greek school to Victoria College as a day boy, where I spent the rest of my schooldays performing in the annual school plays, helping in the library and preparing experiments in the chemistry and physics laboratories. The headmaster, Herbert Barritt, was gentle and considerate, and keen on sport to the extent that cricket and football teams were invited from other cities for matches. There was fencing and boxing, swimming competitions in the large school pool, and the popular cubs for the lower school (sea scouts for the older boys).

In 1949, the English teacher, Mr Porter, produced Shakespeare's play *Julius Caesar*, selecting a number of us – including Hussein of Jordan – to play the parts of the Roman citizens. We had good times during rehearsals twice a week and, during one of them, we were sitting on the floor waiting for Caesar to make his entrance. Hussein was sitting next to me, and his toga slipped while he was getting up – revealing his hairy legs – for some reason, we found this hilarious. Another incident was when a Coptic friend (who was playing Mark Antony), tired of Mr Porter's grumbling at one of the rehearsals, declaimed: "I came to bury Porter, not to praise him!" The yearly school plays were open to the public, and proved very popular with parents and the Alexandrian elite.

On Friday 20 July 1951, King Abdullah I bin al Hussein left Amman with his grandson, Hussein, who was spending his summer holidays in Jordan. On that day, the king decided to pray at the al Aksa mosque in Jerusalem, and asked his grandson to accompany him in full military uniform. That morning, the American ambassador and several politicians advised the king not to visit Jerusalem, as it was rumoured that many Palestinians were unhappy with his decision to start a peace dialogue with Israel. King Abdullah, the sixty-nine-year-old monarch of Jordan, entered the mosque and, after taking a few steps, was shot in the head by a gunman. He fell to the floor, but the assailant – a Palestinian with a criminal record – continued to fire shots all round and one of the bullets struck Prince Hussein's chest on the left side – but, because he was wearing his medals, they saved his life. Hussein was traumatised by the assassination of his grandfather, whom he loved dearly and who was his role model of a king. The royal family and their advisers decided that Hussein should leave Victoria College in Alexandria and continue his education at Harrow in England. The following year, his father, King Talal (who had succeeded Abdullah), was taken ill, declared incapable of ruling the country, and Hussein was crowned king of Jordan.

On returning home from school after hearing the news, my thoughts were of what a king could do at the age of sixteen – could he become a good ruler and not turn out to be like King Farouk? In fact, Hussein developed into an extraordinary king: strong, effective, politically astute, sensitive and caring, especially about his own people and the plight of the Palestinian refugees who were living in Jordan. King Hussein, with his expressive face, always with a smile and soft voice, was a popular monarch and respected throughout the world. Queen Elizabeth II would later invite him to Buckingham Palace when he was in London.

Victoria College had pupils of all nationalities and different religions. European monarchies – Saxe-Coburgs, Glucksburgs and Zogos – rubbed shoulders with Hashemites – the al Sharifs of Arabia and the Mahdis of Sudan – all living together in cosmopolitan Alexandria. The school motto, taken from the 4th century CE's Roman-Alexandrian poet Claudius Claudianus, was *Cuncti Gens Una Sumus* ("we are all one people"). If this motto was applied in the Middle East and the European Union, we would have a more peaceful world and a better future for our children.

My two maternal aunts lived in a pleasant villa on the east of the city, in the district of Cleopatra, running a *haute couture* business. The elder sister had worked for a French fashion house, progressing to having Queen Farida (the first wife of King Farouk) as a client for her summer clothes. A sign that Alexandria was declining was that even this fashion business had to close down; her husband lost his job in the tourist industry and they had no option but to leave, with their seven-year-old daughter, to live in Melbourne, Australia. The younger sister and her husband (my father's younger brother), a retired broker at Alexandria's Cotton Exchange, went to live in Athens.

My mother and her sisters had a French education but lived like the British, having afternoon tea and, once a month, a cocktail party for clients and relatives. In general, most of the foreign girls had a French education but the majority of boys went to English schools.

At medical school, I became friends with Steve Papastephanou, a Greek student from Cairo, who surprised me one day when he sat in front of a piano and played *Etudes* and *Mazurkas* by Chopin, and Rachmaninoff preludes, with dexterity and passion. He had taken lessons from Ignace Tiegerman, a Polish Jew who had escaped from Nazi-occupied Europe and came to live and work in Cairo. When Steve left for the United States for postgraduate studies, he continued to have piano lessons despite his busy surgical career. After his retirement, he participated in several classical music competitions in France.

Tiegerman ran a private music school in Cairo that was popular with the middle classes, both Egyptians and foreigners. He was a graceful and technical performer who fascinated the music lovers of the city. In the music school, there was a Palestinian refugee, Edward Said, who was one of the first to leave Egypt for the United States and studied in New York. He became a professor of English and comparative literature, and a famous author of politically-important cultural books: *The Question of Palestine, Orientalism, Culture and Imperialism* and *Musical Elaborations*. In the United States, he befriended Daniel Barenboim, the internationally-famous pianist and conductor. They established the West-Eastern Divan Orchestra in order to bring young musicians together from Egypt, Israel, Palestine, Syria and Arab countries, hoping that music would heal the wounds of the very painful Israeli–Palestinian conflict. Whilst Edward Said was developing his brand of enlightened internationalism, Egypt was heading in a different direction – anti-western and nationalistic, with a military regime.

Michael Shaloub was a pupil of Lebanese–Syrian descent at the Victoria College in Cairo – the world knows him as "Omar Sharif". David Lean, the British film director, chose him to play an Arab chieftain named Sherif Ali in the film *Lawrence of Arabia*, based on the life of T. E. Lawrence, soldier and scholar, who fought and played a significant role in the Arab struggle against the Ottoman Turks. Lawrence supported the fair distribution of Arab land, and was the last British liberal hero and prophet of decolonisation. His book,

Seven Pillars of Wisdom, is the true story of the Arab struggle.

After completing my medical studies and a year of residency at the University Hospital in Alexandria, it became obvious that foreign doctors could not practice and live under a regime that confiscated their properties. After discussing my career prospects with my parents, we came to a decision for me to go to England, as I had a British education and it was closer for visiting each other. In November 1962, I left Alexandria for London with a sense of relief, mingled with sadness at having to leave my parents behind, who had made the decision to stay for the rest of their lives in the city where they were born. Although their standard of living had declined, they had a reasonable life in the same eastern district, Laurens, close to the sea, and the warm weather that they were used to.

Most of my friends – Copts, Greeks and Jews – left Alexandria with their families within a few years, and spread around the world. It was a high price for all of us to pay.

After working in England, impressed by Britain's National Health Service with its caring medical and nursing staff and cooperative patients, it was obvious to me that this was the country where I wanted to practice and, for thirty-seven years, my professional life was fulfilled and enjoyable.

In Alexandria in the 1950s, before the military revolution, there were 195,000 foreigners; by 1993, the number of foreign residents had dropped to 1,500, and fewer than eight hundred remained in the city by 2012. The foreign communities left behind well-established hospitals, institutions, manufacturing industries, successful printing businesses and shops – the legacy of their time in the city. The multi-ethnic, influential, polyglot community of Alexandria, with its influence on culture and socio-economics, had been eclipsed for ever.

CHAPTER TEN

Four Years of Uncertainty, 1952–1956

From early January 1952, the foreign communities and educated Egyptians were growing anxious at the frequent nationalistic uprisings against the presence of British forces in Alexandria and the Suez Canal zone, accusing the king and the government of not taking any action. It was clear that a political storm was gathering and, on 23 July 1952, the "Free Officer" military revolutionary forces, led by General Mohammed Naguib, took over the country, forced the abdication of King Farouk and dissolved the government in a bloodless coup. Although the British and Americans had remained impartial whilst this military movement was gaining momentum, it later became known that America's Central Intelligence Agency (CIA) station chief in Egypt, Kermit Roosevelt, had secretly supported the "Free Officers" whilst pretending to be a defender of the monarchy.

Regardless of the military revolution, American officials were anxious to resolve the Anglo-Egyptian deadlock that had occurred as a result of Britain's insistence on maintaining troops in the Suez Canal zone. The United States were prepared to financially help the leaders of the revolution, but the British were opposed to the idea of American aid to the military regime.

The "Free Officers" movement was formed in 1949, with General Naguib as president, Colonel Gamal Abdel Nasser as secretary, Abdel Hakim Amer as head of the armed forces, Anwar Sadat (who succeeded Nasser after his death) and other prominent army officers. It was Colonel Abdel Nasser who had masterminded the military coup to free Egypt from its monarchy and the British presence. An agreement for the evacuation of British troops was signed in 1953, which should have calmed the military regime and the Egyptian people.

It was evident from the national newspapers, and from conversations with Egyptian friends, that there was a struggle for power between General Naguib and Colonel Nasser. General Naguib was the figurehead for the first two years, but the real leader had always been Colonel Nasser. Egyptian nationalism was gaining power day by day, and many people from the foreign communities were preparing to leave the country. The Jews were the first to leave, followed by the Italians, Armenians and Maltese, but the main exodus of the largest community in Alexandria – the Greeks – came later.

The attitude of ordinary Egyptians, who had always been friendly to the foreigners, began to change. Even their dress code moved from European clothes towards the *galabeya* (long robes), and women started covering their heads, but not their faces, making a statement that they were Arabs.

The promenade seemed busier, with increased traffic along the carriageway; the buses were so packed that people were hanging from the doors and standing on the rear bumper, while private cars, taxis and the romantic, hooded, horse-drawn carriages were in great demand. It seemed that the uncertainty of the country's politics was making its citizens restless and uncertain about their livelihoods, and they felt the need to get away from the city and go to their villages, clearing the shops of their produce.

Across from the promenade stood blocks of high-rise apartments, neoclassical buildings, European-style houses, shops, restaurants and cafe-bars. The traditional belly-dancing clubs, the KitKat and the Beba Club, seemed to be deserted. The advertising slogans on the billboards that had been mostly in English – "Stella Beer", "Bed and Breakfast", "Chesterfield Cigarettes", "Royal Chocolate" and "Etam Nylons" – gradually changed into Arabic script. Even the music, heard from radios in homes, shops and cafes, changed from English or French to Arabic popular songs.

In early October, the radio announced that Nasser was coming to Alexandria to speak at a rally of ten thousand Egyptian workers. He had always felt comfortable in the city as he had been born in the eastern suburb of Bakos, where his father had been a postman and had married the daughter of a local merchant.

Two Egyptian Christian friends were coming to my home to have a snack and listen to Nasser's speech on the radio. During the first part of the speech, we heard the noise of gunshots. The commentator said that there was pandemonium and, in a loud, emotional voice, said that the gunman who had shot at Nasser had been arrested. After a very brief pause, Nasser spoke in a crystal-clear voice: "My life is yours, my blood is sacrificed for Egypt" (translated from the Arabic), and went on with his speech for ninety minutes.

Three days later, it was announced on the radio and in the newspapers that the person who had attempted to assassinate Nasser was a member of the Muslim Brotherhood. A month later, there were further announcements and reports that six members of the Brotherhood had been found guilty and executed.

For Nasser to retain control of the security services and state administration, he had to convince the people that he was their "true leader" – over the years, he developed a mastery of mass propaganda and passionate oration. It became obvious that Nasser had elements of an autocratic leader who wanted total loyalty and obedience from everyone. President Naguib made an unacceptable political mistake when he expressed his views on the Anglo-Egyptian agreement in a private memorandum to the Revolutionary Command Council and the Muslim Brotherhood – who circulated it in their journal without permission – for this "political bungle", Naguib was removed as leader and placed under house arrest.

Overall, 1954 was an eventful year, with rapid changes in the political life of Egypt but, despite all this, our daily lives were not seriously affected – we continued our studies and tried to enjoy ourselves at the weekends. Naguib resigned, and Nasser was elected president of Egypt, becoming the "undisputed leader of the country".

The American ambassador to Egypt, Jefferson Caffery – a man who understood Egyptian and Middle Eastern politics – offered the military regime a "package", starting with a grant of ten million dollars and a promise to finance the proposed new Aswan Dam. This Aswan project was very important for Egypt, as it would control the Nile floods, reclaim 1.5 million acres of land and generate electricity for Upper Egypt. The Americans were forward-thinking, hoping to improve relations with the Egyptians and the neighbouring Arab world.

Winston Churchill was displeased with the plans of the United States and sent a written plea to the president to suspend their aid. The British concern was not without cause as, one day, the military aid offered by the United States could be turned against the British forces in Egypt. To function properly, the Suez Canal required a military presence as it was easily accessible and could be taken over by other powers.

In late 1954, American officials thought that they were close to a compromise with the Egyptian regime, but Nasser was now "trading" in another direction, turning against the British and Europeans, and negatively influencing the Arabs and North Africans. In his annual speech, on the day of the anniversary of the revolution, Nasser proclaimed that

"Arabs should unite to one nation and help the Algerian rebellion against the French."

Most Arab leaders disapproved of Nasser speaking on their behalf, but there were many others, from African and Asian countries, who considered him as the new leader of the Arab world. He gained support from Communist China, and had meetings with their leader, Zhou Enlai. Two other leaders – Josip Broz Tito of Yugoslavia and India's Prime Minister Jawaharlal Nehru – encouraged him and stressed the importance of "positive neutralism": a doctrine that emphasised non-alignment – with either the West or the Soviet Union.

Britain's Prime Minister Anthony Eden visited Egypt in the hope of finding a working compromise regarding the Suez Canal but, unfortunately, the talks ended abruptly because of a badly-timed attack by Israeli forces on an outpost near Gaza that killed thirty Egyptian soldiers. Until now, no one knows why this incident happened, unless it was planned to disrupt the American–British "deal" with Egypt. The attack demonstrated that Egypt's borders were unprotected and, for the first time, the Soviet Union offered Nasser military support. The "ball game" had now started – the United States and Britain were concerned at the possibility of Soviet Union interference in the Middle East, while the Egyptians were pleased to have both financial help from America and military support from the Soviet Union.

The World Bank came onto the scene, offering Egypt seventy million pounds to fund the proposed Aswan Dam project, but this was not enough – Nasser was asking for 1.3 billion pounds. When the World Bank refused, Nasser adopted a negative attitude and rejected all further offers from the United States, feeling full of himself for knowing that he had the support of the Soviet Union.

Throughout the history of the Arab world, political problems had always been solved with the help of money from western countries but, this time, Nasser was not prepared to accept western aid. The British secret services decided that a solution would be to replace Nasser, and the CIA reported that the British had already taken steps "to bring Nasser down". On hearing of this plan, American Secretary of State John Foster Dulles cancelled all meetings and made no further contact with Egypt.

In 1956, although Nasser should have been pleased that the British troops were finally leaving Egypt, he had an outburst of anger and nationalised the Suez Canal. He knew only too well that it was an illegal act, as the canal was owned by an Anglo-French company. The nationalisation of the Suez Canal sent shock waves through the world, and it seemed unbelievable that the secret services of Britain and the United States had no prior information about the scheme, which the western media called "Nasser's theft".

The closure of the canal caused huge practical and financial problems to the world, as two-thirds of all the oil required by western Europe had to pass through the canal, as well as over one-quarter of all imports to Britain from the Far East. In Alexandria, we had plenty of petrol for cars, yet Great Britain experienced fuel rationing for some time.

The foreign communities were in turmoil, worried about their safety and their livelihoods. Nasser had repeatedly reassured the Alexandrian Greeks that they would not be affected by the nationalisation programme, as he only considered the British, French and Jews to be Egypt's enemies. It was naïve of the Greeks to trust Nasser, who deceived them and continued to nationalise businesses and properties, also damaging his own interests by creating unemployment and destroying the revenue from cotton exports. The Egyptians turned their back on Europe and the West, looking inwards and isolating themselves but, of course, this situation could not last. After Nasser's death, Anwar Sadat started negotiations with Europe and Israel and, after his assassination by the Muslim Brotherhood, Egypt's President Hosni Mubarak became an ally of the West.

CHAPTER ELEVEN

The Suez Canal War

The Suez Canal was constructed to connect the Mediterranean to the Red Sea, allowing ships to considerably shorten their journey from Europe to Asia by avoiding going around Africa via the Cape of Good Hope. The canal was built by the French and opened in 1869; its ownership had been in the hands of the British and French for eighty-seven years. Initially, when the canal was opened, the company had given Egypt's leader, Khedive Ismail, millions of shares. When he ran short of money, he sold the shares to the British government, meaning that the canal was entirely Anglo-French in both ownership and management.

On 26 July 1956, in a two-hour radio broadcast from the "Bourse" Cotton Exchange in Alexandria, President Nasser announced to the world that he had just "nationalised the canal". This shocked the world, as many countries realised the impact that this act would have on their economies.

The American Federal Bureau of Investigation (FBI) sent information to the Intelligence Advisory Committee that Israel was preparing to invade Egypt. The United States was concerned that the use of force in Egypt would be a wrong move, sparking more nationalism and uprisings throughout the Arab world, and providing a good excuse for the Soviet Union to gain a footing in the Middle East. Anthony Eden, British prime minister at the time, failed to inform the United States – his closest ally – that Britain and France were preparing to take back the Suez Canal by force, leaving President Eisenhower "in the dark". Up until the very start of the war, Israel, France and Britain denied that they had any plans to invade Egypt.

The United States leadership was distracted by the Soviet attack in Hungary. At the same time, there was another incident in the Middle East when Israeli military forces seemed to be mobilising towards Jordan but, in fact, they were heading towards Gaza and Sinai, which they conquered within two days.

During the crucial months of September and October 1956, Prime Minister Eden was unwell with attacks of pain and fever arising from complications of previous gall-bladder surgery in 1953. A few days before the closure of the canal, Eden was reported to be taking pain-killing drugs that could have affected his judgement. On 5 October 1956, he accepted a proposal by Israel and France to invade Port Said and recapture the canal. It is quite possible that, if Eden had been well or if he had resigned on medical grounds, the Suez War would not have taken place.

After hearing that Israel had invaded Egypt on 29 October 1956, Eisenhower went immediately to the United Nations, making it clear that the United States did not condone the use of force and declaring: "We must do everything to stop this aggression."

On 31 October 1956, British and French planes bombed Egyptian military posts and airfields around Port Said – in retaliation, the Egyptians sank ships to block the canal entrance. American reconnaissance flights over Syria reported more than 250,000 troops from the Soviet Union and China, and fighter jets were visible at airfields.

The foreign communities of Alexandria were split into two: some were pessimistic that the war would drag on, with disastrous effects, while others were optimistic that it would not last and life would return to normal. As students, we guessed that the next few years would probably be safe but, in the long term, the chance of a good future for everyone was coming to an end. Nasser was a strong leader at the beginning and did not show any anti-western feelings but, gradually, he turned against the British, and then the United States, who had been helpful without entertaining thoughts of colonisation.

The western powers were concerned about the Soviet Union obtaining a presence in the Suez Canal zone, and it was becoming obvious that Nasser was politically confused on important issues, having no experienced advisers to help him deal with the politicians of the West. By his closure of the Suez Canal, he created a serious worldwide crisis without having any idea of the long-term consequences of his action.

As medical students, we decided to offer ourselves to the country at war, and a few of us from the foreign communities volunteered for the "Home Guard". On the day we enlisted, they gave us a military uniform and sent us to an officer to instruct us on the use of a Bren gun, how to assemble it from four pieces, and how to use it – initially, without bullets! Everything was moving so fast; the following three mornings, we went for training and, when the officers considered us capable, we were stationed on the seacoast next to the eastern harbour.

Surprisingly, we were not worried at all, enjoyed the training and our guard duties and, as we saw no action, found the whole experience exciting rather than frightening. The hundreds of soldiers who were stationed along the coast were told to expect parachutists and enemy landings from the sea, and large guns were placed at strategic positions. This did not happen and, in fact, there was no attack on the city.

At night, when we were hungry, we would go across the road to where there was a taverna, well-known for its grilled meats. My favourite was the liver served with pitta bread; this was my first "takeaway", and we all sat by the harbour eating, while scanning the sky and the sea. We heard stories that there were casualties on both sides, and that British and

French troops had occupied Port Said, but overseas news was censored. The United States, the Soviet Union and influential British politicians – Rab Butler, Harold Macmillan and Labour leader Hugh Gaitskell – demanded the withdrawal of forces, calling the war the "Eden-Mollet folly". There was no doubt that international pressure was being applied to stop the war and force the withdrawal of the British, French and Israeli troops.

On 5 November 1956, at the time of the landing of the Anglo-French troops at Port Said, Nasser delivered a speech from Al Azhar University in Cairo. Six weeks later, on 23 December 1956 (arranged to coincide with the withdrawal of the enemy forces), he gave his "victory speech" at the same university. By that time, Nasser had become an accomplished orator, frequently using emotional phrases such as "the city of Port Said is honoured for the blood lost for the sake of Egypt's survival," and "the defeat of the imperialists by an unprepared country such as ours". The uneducated Egyptians did not read newspapers or magazines – they only listened to the radio – so the speeches were very important to impress the masses with his achievements. Despite the fact that the Egyptian forces had been defeated and most of their military equipment destroyed, Nasser turned the conflict into a personal victory, convincing everyone that he had "freed the Arab world from western imperialists" – a theme that he adopted throughout his eighteen years of leadership.

Nasser was the most important leader in the modern history of Egypt and the Arab world, and he swayed the masses by his broadcasts, with his speeches lasting for more than two hours and mesmerising the public.

Two weeks after the invasion, it was becoming obvious that the withdrawal of troops would be inevitable and the fighting would stop. The United States was relieved when Nasser reported to their ambassador that he had refused Soviet military support. One did not need to know much about politics to realise that a war in the Middle East could ruin the West's relations with Egypt and its neighbouring countries, and further inflame the Israeli–Palestinian conflict.

As there was no action in Alexandria, those of us in the "Home Guard" returned our uniforms and guns. The British had announced that they would withdraw their military forces by 23 December 1956 and, by 1st December, the university had reopened and we went back to our studies.

Anthony Eden resigned on 9 January 1957, with Harold Macmillan replacing him as prime minister. Life at medical school did not change: the lectures continued in English, the majority of the teaching and senior staff had received their postgraduate training in Britain, they were gentle to patients, and the standard of medicine in Alexandria was very high. The medical school and the teaching hospital were built on the site of the ancient Greek theatre and, from the cafeteria and the restaurant, we had limited but attractive views of the coastal promenade and the Mediterranean Sea.

However, everyday life for both Egyptians and foreigners was deteriorating – there was a reduction of imports from Europe and the cotton industry had come to a halt. The "Bourse" Cotton Exchange closed down, and we were told that the Arab petrol-producing countries had reduced the supply of petrol to Britain and France. The cinemas continued to work but showed only old films, and the cafeterias and restaurants took some time to return to their previous "cosmopolitan" service. Most of the foreign schools closed down – even Victoria College was forced to change its name to "Victory College". Only Egyptian and Arab pupils were allowed to be enrolled, with the exception of one Jewish boy who was allowed to stay for a year, and then left for the United States where he wrote a book called *Out of Egypt*. The military regime stated that all teaching must be changed from English into Arabic, which was not a sensible act and a backward step for education, as English was the second language of the whole of the Middle East.

Despite the disturbance to our family life and uncertainty for our future, we decided to have our New Year's Eve party, "Reveillon", in the villa of our Coptic friends, Assad and Sami, who were two of the nicest friends that we had had in our group for more than six years. Every Christmas and New Year, their parents left to spend the winter in Upper Egypt where the weather was warmer, and we were lucky to have their cook and maid at our disposal. We were a group of sixteen and had a Grundig record player with a good collection of 78s. It is interesting that we still remember most of them: from England, Acker Bilk; from America, Bing Crosby, Frank Sinatra, Dean Martin and Bill Haley and the Comets; from France, Edith Piaf, Gilbert Becaud and Dalida; from Italy, Renato Carosone and Domenico Modugnio; and from Greece, George Guetari and Sophia Vembo. We had a wonderful time, danced a lot and ended the party at 12:45 a.m. (as some friends needed to catch the last tram home), after a cheek-to-cheek dance on the veranda under the stars to Nat King Cole's *Let's fall in love*.

During the first months of 1957, Nasser put forward his socialist programme, incorporating the nationalisation of foreign assets and a new system of appointing Egyptians, from either the civil service or army, as co-directors of businesses. My father ran a small company and accepted these new laws with resignation and humour; his way of dealing with the new regime. The economic policy of the military was to bring businesses under state ownership – a revolutionary change for a modern country. Many of the wealthy landowners and cotton merchants were financially devastated, and many Copts left Egypt for Canada. The Egyptians themselves had to stay, so moved to smaller houses and apartments, having lost their land and villas.

The nationalisation of businesses and the confiscation of land was an easy way to get rid of the foreign communities and fill the regime's coffers under the banner of socialism.

The British, French and Jews were wary of Nasser from the very start, and they were proved to be right. A relevant comment about Nasser came from Sir Robert Menzies, an experienced politician and prime minister of Australia who visited Egypt in 1956, before the Suez crisis, and reported his thoughts to Anthony Eden, describing Nasser as "a likeable fellow, but lacking in experience and his logic did not travel far".

For five years after 1957, Nasser raged a propaganda war against King Hussein of Jordan to try and overthrow the monarchy; fortunately, this failed, but angered many in the Middle East, including us, who loved and admired our schoolmate for the way he was handling his country, which had a huge Palestinian refugee population that created political imbalance, fragility and financial difficulties. Sadly, Jordan had no oil revenues.

Eighteen months after the Suez War, it seemed that social life in Alexandria was slowly recovering for the Egyptians, but it was becoming increasingly obvious that there would be a mass exodus of Europeans within a few years. This was something that would leave a huge gap in many areas, particularly cotton export, and would affect employment for the Egyptians who worked in industries owned by foreigners.

The United States was supportive of the Egyptian military regime from 1952, offering economic help – which was refused. After the invasion, President Eisenhower appealed to the United Nations, insisting on the total withdrawal of troops, and Nasser had no reason to be "anti-American".

With the passage of time, attitudes changed and the United States became more supportive of Israel – which concerned many in the Middle East and Muslims worldwide. Reaction started with the emergence of the Palestinian

Liberation Organisation (PLO), then the growth of the Muslim Brotherhood in Egypt and its Palestinian offshoot, Hamas, followed much later, in 1982, by Hezbollah – a Shi'a Islamic militant group supported by Iran and Syria.

Around 1988, al Qaeda emerged in Afghanistan as a multinational terrorist group of radical Sunni origin that spread to Yemen, the Middle East, Somalia, and West and Central Africa, with terrorist acts being carried out world-wide – increasing after the United States invaded Iraq. This unrest has had far-reaching consequences: the Israeli–Palestinian conflict needs to be resolved – not by Britain, France or the United States as there is evidence to show that their previous efforts have failed – but by the United Nations.

CHAPTER TWELVE

The Decline of Modern Alexandria

There are several reasons for the decline of the modern city: a young, inexperienced king, fervent nationalism, poor politics, incompetent leaders and the inability of western rulers to understand the problems that Egypt was facing at that time. King Farouk, the last monarch, was without doubt responsible for the demise of his country. He reigned from 1936 until 1952, manipulated by his prime ministers, palace staff and the British diplomats in Egypt.

Before the Second World War, Farouk was briefly pro-Nazi, to the extent that he accepted a gift from Adolf Hitler – a custom-built, convertible Mercedes. His Italian barber and intimate friend, Pietro della Valle, was the procurer of women to keep the king amused. Farouk's mistresses included high-society ladies, British, French and Jewish commoners, and popular Egyptian belly dancers of the time. He befriended Edmond Galhan, an undercover Lebanese arms dealer acting as an importer of fountain pens, who proved to be the king's downfall, having sold defective weapons to the Egyptian army for an unnecessary war against Israel in 1948. This war was a catastrophic defeat for Egypt, and Farouk became an unacceptable monarch. This combination of a humiliating defeat, loss of respect from the people of the country and sixty years of British domination made the time rife for Egyptian nationalism.

In the early 1900s, there were two significant events that occurred outside of Egypt that changed the lives of the people and had long-standing repercussions. The first was the Sykes–Picot agreement of May 1916, to "cut up" the Arab world by creating the new countries of Lebanon, Jordan, Palestine and Israel from what had previously been part of Syria. Syria opposed these independent states, considering the agreement to be a violation of its territorial integrity. The British would govern Iraq, Palestine and Jordan, while the French would have a mandate over Lebanon and Syria. In the Arabian Peninsula, semi-desert territories such as Hegaz in the west, in areas along the Red Sea as far south as Yemen and, in the east, Nazd by the Persian Gulf, were given independent status although they had small populations. It is reported by George Antonius (a British diplomat who served in the British Mandate Administration in Palestine and one of the first historians of Arab nationalism) that, as early as 1918, Sir Mark Sykes recognised the error of his judgement and urged, for the sake of peace, that the British should review "Arab civilisation and unity and prepare them for ultimate independence" – but his warning went unheeded.

The second event was the Balfour Declaration of 1917: a British promise to the worldwide Jewish communities of the creation of a homeland for them in Palestine. Thousands of years ago, the small region west of the Jordan river and south of Mount Hermon was called Philistine, where Goliath fought David in biblical times. British diplomats and scholars did not like this name, so looked through some ancient Greek books and decided on the name "Palestine". In the early 1900s, the population of Palestine was 92 percent Arab. After the British crushed the Arab revolt of 1936, and the Israelis defeated the invading Arab forces in 1948, Jewish immigration accelerated and Israel was in possession of 78 percent of British Mandatory Palestine.

The Middle East problems created economic and political difficulties: the Egyptians lost the war of 1948, there

were thousands of refugees and, as only Alexandria and
Cairo had Arab universities, it became impossible to
educate everyone.

The PLO was crafted by Egypt's military leaders –
Gamal Abdel Nasser supported Yassir Arafat as leader in
Palestine. The Muslim Brotherhood evolved in Cairo in
1928, and produced a terrorist offshoot, Hamas, which
made the Palestinians an international force in worldwide
terrorism. In 1948, an organisation calling itself the "Free
Officers" emerged within the Egyptian army, some of
whom were sympathisers of the Muslim Brotherhood (*al
Ikhwan al Muslimin*), a secret society of radical Islamic
fundamentalists. The Muslim Brotherhood was founded by
an ascetic leader, Hassan al Banna, as a peaceful movement
but, within twenty years, it gradually changed into an
Islamic terrorist group with a membership of more than half
a million – the organisation survived politically with the
support of some ministers in the Egyptian government. It
has been alleged that Hassan al Banna was assassinated on
the orders of King Farouk.

A political question that needs to be asked is why some
leaders destroy their own society – is it due to holding onto
power for too long, use of their position only for financial
gain, or inexperience and lack of awareness of the consequences of their actions? In modern politics, society
declines if there is a failure to make group decisions by
allowing only the leader's opinion to prevail, which
commonly occurs in undemocratic or theocratic regimes.

Nasser's personality was such that he rarely listened to
advice, and had neither real knowledge of international
affairs nor experience to deal with the politicians of the
western world. After the disaster of the Suez War, Nasser
shut down the "Bourse" Cotton Exchange – a serious
mistake, as it had been successfully run by both Egyptians
and foreigners. The closure was responsible for the decline
of cotton trading over several decades.

When Britain, France and Israel decided to invade the Suez Canal, they failed to consider the likely consequences of their actions. All that the war did was to create economic chaos and more tension between the West and the Arab world. The mistake of the West in starting wars continues to this day, with devastating effects on economies, causing more unrest throughout the Middle East – and more terrorism.

After the Suez conflict, the first to have their businesses confiscated were the British, French and Jews and, by 1957, most of the foreign communities had started to leave the country. There was a serious reduction in imported foreign goods – but no shortage of alcoholic drinks, as they were distilled locally.

Before the Suez War, the cinemas had always played an important part in the entertainment of the city but, during and after the war, they showed only Egyptian films, or old American and British movies, and there were no opera performances or orchestral concerts from abroad.

The French names of squares and streets were changed to Arabic, and the standard of living dropped, with an unacceptable level of unemployment and a worrying increase in the number of beggars in the streets and outside the shops. The restaurants and cafes experienced a sharp reduction as most of their customers had been Europeans. Quoting from Durrell's book, "the city of five races, five languages and a dozen creeds" that lived harmoniously together, no longer existed.

By 1961, 90 percent of the foreigners had left Egypt, having lost their properties, businesses and money. The less well-off lost their jobs, and everyone had to start life again on the other side of the world, learning to adapt to a different way of life in a new country.

In 1993, the Egyptian Ministry of Defence invited me to demonstrate new orthopaedic techniques in the Military Hospital in Cairo, as I had trained several Egyptian surgeons in Birmingham, England. Whilst in Cairo, a colleague suggested that we should visit Alexandria together. We spent two days there but, sadly, I did not feel comfortable in the city where I had been born, and preferred Cairo as it was more friendly and hospitable, with a cosmopolitan flavour similar to that which I had experienced in Alexandria as a young man.

The Alexandrian Corniche (coastal promenade), where I had walked endlessly in the 1950s, had not changed much, but the city was crammed with new, ugly, high-rise buildings masking the old, attractive, neoclassical houses. Many homes and villas were neglected, decaying with broken windowsills and shutters and, at the back of these buildings, there were mounds of garbage and dirty roads. The popular beaches of Stanley Bay, San Stefano, Sidi Bishr and Montazah were still there, but the sandy beaches were not clean, littered with empty bottles, discarded papers and rotten fruit. The city had lost its foreign inhabitants, plus the tourists, writers, poets and travellers who had a romantic view of Alexandria and regarded the city as their "muse". The Egyptian military regime turned its back on the Mediterranean world and the rest of Europe to become inward-looking.

Alexandria is a casualty of Egyptian nationalism, the failure of Britain and the United States to stabilise the country, the Suez War and Nasser's vengeful desire to get rid of the foreign communities. The Egyptians are gentle people and hospitable; those living in the cities are well educated, hard-working, have a good sense of humour and the majority are peaceful. I have personal experience of this, having lived with them from childhood until the age of twenty-six.

The Muslim Brotherhood did not attack westerners but targeted their own politicians and leaders – in 1945, they executed Prime Minister Ahmed Maher, in 1948, Prime Minister Noqrashi and, in 1949, the chief of Cairo's police.

Nasser escaped assassination but, in 1981, they killed Anwar Sadat – the president who succeeded Nasser – for trying to negotiate with Israel for peace and cooperation.

Whilst living in England, I kept an interest in the life of Alexandria, and learnt that one-third of all the industrial output of Egypt goes through its port. On the west of Alexandria is Mex, where there are paper mills, an asphalt industry, limestone quarries, salt production, tanning factories and oil refineries. This means that there must be sufficient money being generated that could be used for the needs of the city to improve its infrastructure and tourism.

For many years, there had been talk of building a library in Alexandria to try and replace the ancient state-funded Grand Library of the Greek Ptolemies, but the major discussion was always whether a city that had so many problems could properly support such a grandiose project or whether the money should be used to improve the city's housing for its ever-increasing population. In the late 1990s, the British "Friends of the Alexandria Library" asked me for a donation, which was given willingly. This project was funded by Arab countries, many European governments, individuals from around the world and UNESCO. "Bibliotheca Alexandrina" was completed and opened in 2002.

During the same year, Alexandria honoured the founder of the city – Alexander the Great – and a bronze equestrian statue was placed in the vicinity of the Shallalat Gardens in Chatby. All of the money had been raised by alumni of the Greek High Schools and Greek expatriates. The charitable organisation of Alexander S. Onassis is considering renovating the neoclassical villa in the Antoniades Gardens, by the Smouha district, to be used as a centre for Alexandrian and Mediterranean studies and research. It is our hope that, if this project happens, this attractive building will not be occupied by civil servants cataloguing books and concerned with mundane problems. A practical idea is to invite scholars from around the world to research, to teach hiero-glyphics and ancient Greek, and to decipher the papyri found in Egypt instead of having to send them to various universities in Britain, Europe and the United States for study – and to wait years for their return.

The city needs reconstruction by renovating the old neoclassical buildings and villas. This can only be achieved if the gates of Alexandria are opened to European manu-facturers and businessmen, who would also bring with them their style of life. It needs the desire and enthusiasm of the people, the guidance of the Egyptian authorities and of multicultural experts. In our 21st century CE, maybe the winds of change could slowly bring people together again to work for peace and improve the standard of living by bringing prosperity to its citizens.

The years have gone so fast, and the Alexandria that I had known is so different – and I have grown old. But, in my mind, the city will always be as it was before the Egyptian military revolution, when a young man of any race could have a good education, enjoy his life, watch the latest Hollywood and European movies, go to a concert or club and catch the eye of a multi-ethnic or Egyptian girl.

Before leaving Alexandria to return home to England, I walked a short distance along the coastal promenade. It was a melancholic evening: across the road were the shops, cafe-terias and restaurants, but I heard no music, neither Arabic nor European. The sky was dark, there were no stars and no moon, and I finally realised that the cosmopolitan city of yesterday was gone for ever.

The Cover Illustrations

The author is indebted to Peter Seibt for providing the front cover illustration, based on a modern visual interpretation of the Lighthouse of Alexandria, sometimes called the Pharos of Alexandria. The tower was reputed to be 120 metres high, and was started in 270 BC. It was subsequently destroyed by an earthquake in 1303.

The back cover image is of the New Bibliotheca Alexandrina, recently built in honour of the Ancient Library of Alexandria – one of the largest and most significant libraries of the ancient world. It was dedicated to the Muses, the nine goddesses of the arts. The New Library of Alexandria provides bibliographic and multi-media exploration of Egypt's heritage across 5000 years of history, including Ancient Egyptian, Ptolemaic, Hellenistic, Coptic and Muslim heritage.

Select Bibliography

Al Ghitani, G. *Zayni Barakat*. Cairo: The American University Press, 2004.

Andronikos, Manolis. *Vergina: The Royal Tombs and the Ancient City*. Athens: Ekdotike Athenon, 1984.

Antonius, George. *The Arab Awakening: The Story of the Arab Nationalist Movement*. New York: J. B. Lippincott, 1939.

Arrian. *History of Alexander and Indica*. Translated by P. A. Brunt. 2 vols. Loeb Classical Library. Cambridge, MA: Harvard University Press, 1976.

Athenaeus. *Deipnosophistae*. Translated by C. B. Gulick. Vols. 1–3, pp. 315–370. Loeb Classical Library. Cambridge, MA: Harvard University Press, 1927.

Boardman, John, J. Griffin, and O. Murray. *Greece and the Hellenistic World*. The Oxford History of the Classical World. Oxford: Oxford University Press, 1988.

Byron, G. G. *The Works of Lord Byron*. Vol. 1. London: John Murray, 1827.

Cartledge, Paul. *Alexander the Great: The Hunt for a New Past*. London: Pan Macmillan, 2005. New edition, New York: Vintage Books, 2006.

Cassius, D. *The Roman History: The Reign of Augustus*. Translated by I. Scott-Kilvert. London: Penguin, 1987.

Chugg, Andrew. "Alexander's Final Resting Place". *History Today* 54, no. 7 (2004).

Cunliffe, Barry. *The Extraordinary Voyage of Pytheas the Greek: The Man Who Discovered Britain*. London: Penguin, 2003.

Curtius, Quintus. *History of Alexander*. Translated by R. C. Rolfe. Vol. 2. Loeb Classical Library. Cambridge, MA: Harvard University Press, 1936.

Dalby, A. *Siren Feasts: A History of Food and Gastronomy in Greece*. London: Routledge, 1996.

Dallas, R. *King Hussein*. London: Profile Books, 1999.

Dalven, R. *The Complete Poems of Cavafy*. A Harvest Book. New York: Harcourt, 1976.

Durrell, Lawrence G. *The Alexandria Quartet*. 4 vols. London: Faber & Faber, 1962.

Empereur, J. Y., and S. Compoint. *Alexandria Rediscovered*. London: British Museum Press, 1998.

Forster, E. M. *Alexandria: A History and a Guide, and Pharos and Pharillon*. Edited by Miriam Allott. Abinger Edition. London: André Deutsch, 2004.

France, Peter. *Greek as a Treat*. London: BBC Books, 1993.

Fraser, P. M. *Ptolemaic Alexandria*. London: Clarendon Press, 1972.

Goddio, Franck, and M. Clauss. *Egypt's Sunken Treasures*. Berlin: Prestel Books, 2006.

Gombrich, E. H. *The Story of Art*. 16th edition. London: Phaidon Press, 1995.

Green, P. *Alexander to Actium: The Hellenistic Age*. London: Thames & Hudson, 1990.

Gregory, A. *Eureka: The Birth of Science*. London: Icon Books, 2001.

Grosskurth, P. *Byron*. London: Hodder & Stoughton, 1997.

Haag, M. *Alexandria: City of Memory*. Athens: Okeanida, 2005 (Greek).

Hahn, P. L. *The United States, Great Britain and Egypt*. Chapel Hill, NC: University of North Carolina Press, 1991.

Hammond, N. G. L. *The Genius of Alexander the Great*. Translated by P. Theodoris. Thessaloniki: Iris, 2007.

Heath, T. L. *A History of Greek Mathematics*. Vol. 2. London: Clarendon Press, 1921. Dover Edition, 1981.

Homer. *The Iliad, and The Odyssey*. Translated by E. V. Rieu. London: Mackays of Chatham, 1987.

Iliopoulos, G. *The Unknown Alexander*. Athens: Epikinonies, 2003 (Greek).

Keeley, E. *Cafavy's Alexandria*. Princeton, NJ: Princeton University Press, 1996.

Keeley, E., and P. Sherrard. *C. P. Cavafy: Collected Poems*. London: Chatto & Windus, 1990.

Kitroeff, A. *The Greeks in Egypt: Ethnicity and Class*. London: Ithaca Press, 1987.

Laertius, Diogenes. *Lives of Eminent Philosophers*. Translated by R. D. Hicks. Vols. 1–2. Loeb Classical Library. Cambridge, MA: Harvard University Press, 1936.

Lane-Fox, R. *Alexander the Great*. London: Penguin, 1987.

Liddell, R. *Cavafy: A Biography*. London: Gerald Duckworth, 2000.

Lucian. *Works*. Translated A. M. Harmon. Loeb Classical Library. Cambridge, MA: Harvard University Press, 1913.

Lydakis, S. *Ancient Greek Painting*. Los Angeles: Paul Getty Foundation, 2004.

Macleod, R. *The Library of Alexandria*. London: I. B. Tauris, 2004.

Mahfouz, N. *Autumn Quail*. Cairo: The American University Press, 1989.

Mlodinow, L. *Euclid's Window*. London: Penguin, 2001.

Pfrommer, M. *Greek Gold from Hellenistic Egypt*. Los Angeles: Paul Getty Museum Publications, 2002.

Pharsalia, Lucan. *The Civil War*. Translated by J. D. Duff. Loeb Classical Library. Cambridge, MA: Harvard University Press, 1928.

Pliny. *Natural History*. Translated by H. Rackham. Vols. 4–5. Loeb Classical Library. Cambridge, MA: Harvard University Press, 1936.

Plotinos. *The First Ennead*. Translation and comments by P. Kalligas. Athens: Publication Centre of Greek Writers, 1994.

Plutarch. *Plutarch's Lives: Alexander*. Translated by John Dryden. Edited by A. H. Clough. Vol. 4. Boston, MA: Little, Brown & Co., 1888.

Polybius. *The Histories*. Translated by W. R. Paton. Loeb Classical Library. Cambridge, MA: Harvard University Press, 1946.

Ptolemy, Claudius. *Tetrabiblos*. Translated by F. E. Robbins. Loeb Classical Library. Cambridge, MA: Harvard University Press, 1940.

Said, E. W. *Culture and Imperialism*. London: Chatto & Windus, 1993.

Saunders, N. *Alexander's Tomb*. New York: Basic Books, 2006.

Seferis, G. *Poems in Greek*. 15th edition. Athens: Ikaros, 1985.

Siculus, Diodorus. *Library of History*. Translated by R. M. Geer. Book 18. Loeb Classical Library. Cambridge, MA: Harvard University Press, 1967.

Strabo. *Geography*. Translated by H. L. Jones. Loeb Classical Library. Cambridge, MA: Harvard University Press, 1917. Reprinted in 1933.

Suetonius. *Lives of Illustrious Men*. Translated by J. C. Rolfe. Vol. 2. Loeb Classical Library. Cambridge, MA: Harvard University Press, 1914. Revised in 1997.

Topis, A. *Alexandria: Moments, Places and People who Once Lived There*. Athens: Kedros, 2002 (Greek).

Trypanis, C. *The Penguin Book of Greek Verse*. London: Penguin, 1971.

Tsirkas, S. *Cavafy and his Epoch*. Athens: Kedros, 1958.

———. *Drifting Cities*. Translated by K. Cicellis. Athens: Kedros, 1995.

Vatikiotis, P. J. *Nasser: A New Generation*. London: Croom Helm Images, 1978.

Wood, M. *In the Footsteps of Alexander the Great*. London: BBC Books, 1997.

Index

Page numbers in italics refer to maps and photographs.